BOER WAR MEMORABILIA

The Boer War was also known as

ANGLO-BOER WAR
CRYING WAR
FREEDOM WAR
GREAT BOER WAR
LAST COLONIAL WAR
SECOND ANGLO-BOER WAR
SECOND BOER WAR
SECOND SOUTH AFRICAN WAR
SOUTH AFRICAN CAMPAIGN
SOUTH AFRICAN WAR
TRANSVAAL CAMPAIGN
TRANSVAAL WAR

BOER WAR

Pieter Oosthuizen
with the collaboration of Alan Pee

MEMORABILIA

The Alderman Press

Published by The Alderman Press,
1/7, Church Street, Edmonton, N9 9DR
1987

© Pieter Oosthuizen, 1987.

British Library Cataloguing in Publication Data

Oosthuizen, Pieter
  Boer War memorabilia : the collector's
  guide.
  1. Military paraphernalia—Collectors and
  collecting   2. south African war, 1899–1902
  —Equipment—Collectors and collecting
  I. Title
  355.8'09'034   U790

ISBN 0-946619-19-0

All rights reserved. No part of this publication
may be reproduced, stored in a retrieval system, or
transmitted in any form or by any means, electronic,
mechanical, photocopying or otherwise without the prior
permission of the publishers.

The publishers wish to acknowledge and express their thanks
to the following;

for his photographic work	— Chris Halton.
for their editorial endeavours	— Michael Bruff and Julie Nelson.
for design and production	— Bill Antrobus of Deer Park Productions.
for typesetting	— Mathematical Composition Setters, Salisbury.
for origination, printing and binding	— BAS Printers Limited, Over Wallop, Hampshire.

Printed in Great Britain.

'The things, we know, are neither rich nor rare,
The wonder's how the devil they got there!'

Alexander Pope

Contents

Sources and Acknowledgements — ix
Bibliography — xi
Introduction — xiii
Chronological list of major Boer War events — xvii
Alphabetical reference of names and places — xix
Boer War Victoria Cross heroes — xxix
Map of South Africa (1900) — xxxiii

Chapter 1 General Ceramics — 1
            Plates, services, tea-sets, loving cups, mugs, tumblers, tobacco
            jars and general items

Chapter 2 Character Figures, Busts and Statuettes — 35
            Porcelain figures, Staffordshire figures, bisque figures, Goss and
            Parian ware figures

Chater 3   Model Soldiers — 53
            Miniature models

Chapter 4 Glassware — 59
            Plates, glasses, paperweights, rolling-pins and busts

Chapter 5 Stamps and Covers — 65
            Postage stamps, war covers, POW covers, postmarks and censors'
            marks

Chapter 6 Prisoner-of-War Handicraft — 83
            Wood, bone, horn and ivory items and carvings, pipes, textiles,
            metal items and stone carvings

Chapter 7 Coins and Notes — 101

Chapter 8	Gold and Silver Memorabilia and Jewellery	113
Chapter 9	Tin and Pewter Memorabilia	127
Chapter 10	Ephemera Commemorative letters, photographs, maps, newspapers and magazines, cigarette cards, posters, music, postcards, tickets, etchings, caricatures, illustrations, games, sermons, advertisements, announcements, official documents.	137
Chapter 11	Textiles	177
Chapter 12	General Books, medallions, trench souvenirs, knives, ashtrays, umbrella stands, tables, pipes, lapel pins, trivets, viewers and miscellaneous items	189
Chapter 13	One-of-a-kind Collectibles Presentation caskets, paintings and watercolours, etc.	217
Index		231

Sources and Acknowledgements

A great amount of thanks is due to all the people who have given me so much of their time and support while I was researching and gathering information for this book. It is impossible to express thanks to all the people who have shown or expressed kindnesses during the period this book was compiled or during the years in which I acquired my collection. However very special thanks to:

My wife, for all her encouragement and editing;
Mr Alan Peek, USA, for having laid the groundwork for me to write the book;
Mr Kenneth Griffith, London, who unstintingly gave me so much of his time and allowed his collection to be photographed;
Major P. N. Erskine, Stellenbosch in the Cape, who on very short notice made his notes and photographs available to me;
Mr Chris Halton, London, for his excellent photographs;
Mr Peter Johnson, London, Curator of the Forbes Magazine Museum of Military Miniatures, Tangier, Morocco, for his support;
Mr Gerald Hoberman, Cape Town, for offering to make all his photographs available to me;
Superintendent A. Bermingham, Hamilton, Bermuda, who went out of his way to find material for me;
Mr Colin Benbow, Hamilton, Bermuda, for his support.

Many weeks of research work were spent in a number of museums, where, without exception, I found encouragement and support at all levels.
Africana Museum, Johannesburg – with special thanks to Mrs Hillary Bruce;
British Museum Library, London;
City Museum and Art Gallery, Stoke-on-Trent;
Douwe Egberts Museum, Utrecht, The Netherlands;
Imperial War Museum, London;
National Army Museum, London;
National Cultural History and Open Air Museum, Pretoria, with special thanks to Mrs Elda Grobler and Miss H. Turkstra;

National Maritime Museum, Greenwich, London;
Victoria & Albert Museum, London;
War Museum of the Boer Republics, Bloemfontein, with special thanks to Miss Elria Wessels.

In addition I must express a special thanks to all the helpful people in The Scout Association, Baden-Powell House, London.

Grateful thanks also for assistance received from the following:

Phillips Fine Art Auctioneers in London;
Sotheby's in London and Johannesburg;
Antique Collectors' Club Ltd., Woodbridge, Suffolk;
Britannia, Grays Antique Market, London with special thanks to Rita & Ian Smythe;
British Collectibles, First Floor, Georgian Village, Camden Passage, London with special thanks to Dennis Colton, Ron Gough and Roy Busby;
Gilda Conrich, The Mall, Camden Passage, London;
The Pipe Shop, Antiquarius, London with special thanks to Brian Tipping.
Catherine Alder, First Floor, Georgian Village, Camden Passage, London.

Bibliography

A. Conan Doyle, *The Great Boer War*
Barbara Morris, *Victorian Table Glass and Ornaments*
Byron Farwell, *The Great Anglo-Boer War*
Colin Benbow, *Boer Prisoners of War in Bermuda*
Christiaan Rudolf de Wet, *Three Years' War*
Deneys Reitz, *Commando*
Johannes Meintjes, *The Anglo-Boer War 1899–1902. A Pictorial History*
Kenneth Griffith and Edward B. Proud, *History of British Army Postal Service*
Ken Jacobs, *Coins of South Africa*
Matthy Esterhuysen, *Our Money Heritage (Ons Gelderfenis)*
Matthy Esterhuysen, *Commemorative Medals in Honour of President S. J. P. Kruger*
National Cultural History and Open Air Museum, *A Musical Laurel to the Boers (1899–1902) ('n Musikale Lourierkrans vir die Boere 1899–1902)*
N. Hudson Moore, *Old Pewter, Brass, Copper and Sheffield Plate*
Pamela Todd and David Fordham, *Private Tucker's Boer War Diary*
Peter Johnson, *Toy Armies*
P. D. Gordon Pugh, *Staffordshire Portrait Figures*
Phillip A. Watkins, *The History of the Victoria Cross (1904)*
Thomas Pakenham, *The Boer War*

Periodicals & Publications

Antiques in South Africa
Black and White Budget
Catalogue of the Coins of South Africa, 1983 edition, Alec Kaplan
Scotts Standard Postage Stamp Catalogue

Introduction

The collecting of Boer War memorabilia owes its growing popularity to the great cast of personalities who participated in the war, and the electrifying events that took place during the period 1899–1902. These events generated intense emotion and controversy, and large quantities of very varied commemorative items were manufactured at this time, which today provide rewarding collecting in both general and specialised fields.

I would like to give the reader a brief overview of why the Boer War caught the imagination of the international community, both at the time and subsequently.

1. Shortly before the war the greatest gold fields known to man were discovered in the South African Republic (Transvaal).
2. The world's imagination was also captivated by the riches of the diamond fields at Kimberley and the 'Diamond Barons' these diamond fields created.
3. The exploration of the diamond and gold fields drew prospectors and speculators to South Africa from all corners of the earth.
4. The Zulu Wars and the First Boer War also placed South Africa on the front pages of the international press.
5. Soldiers from many countries in the British Empire participated in the Boer War. Apart from all the troops from the home countries and the Southern African colonies, troops from Australia, Burma, Canada, Ceylon, India, New Zealand and Hong Kong participated in the war.
6. There were Americans and Irish fighting on both sides. There were Dutch, French, Germans and Russians fighting with the Boers.
7. There were ambulances and nursing staff from many countries supporting both sides in the war.
8. The Boer War is now considered to be the last colonial war. The South African Republic of President Kruger became the Transvaal Colony and the Orange Free State of President Steyn became the Orange River Colony.
9. The Boer War is considered to be the forerunner of modern warfare. During this war from 1899 to 1902:
    (*a*) trench warfare was initiated;
    (*b*) armoured trains were used;
    (*c*) guerilla warfare was initiated;

(d) balloons were used for communications;
(e) wireless transmission of messages to the war front was introduced.
10. Emotions were also stirred by a number of events:
    (a) the great Sieges of Mafeking and Ladysmith which caught the public's imagination;
    (b) the use of Scouts by Major-General Baden-Powell at Mafeking which led to the formation of the international Scout Association;
    (c) the refugee camps (concentration camps) into which the Boer women and children were herded;
    (d) the scorched earth policy that was implemented in the second stage of the war.
11. Famous writers were involved:
    (a) Rudyard Kipling was a war correspondent;
    (b) Conan Doyle's book *The Great Boer War* caused great controversy.
12. Future statesmen of international repute participated in the war:
    (a) Winston Churchill, the famous wartime Prime Minister of Britain, was a war correspondent in the field;
    (b) Mahatma Gandhi, the pacifist who led India to independence, was a stretcher bearer with General Buller's troops in Natal;
    (c) Louis Botha, the first Prime Minister of the Union of South Africa, was a Boer General;
    (d) Jan Smuts, Prime Minister of South Africa and Field Marshal in the Second World War, was a Boer general.
13. Ambitious and well-known Empire builders had a role in this war:
    (a) Joseph Chamberlain was the Colonial Secretary;
    (b) Cecil John Rhodes played a prominent role;
    (c) Alfred Milner was the High Commissioner for South Africa.
14. The end of the Victorian era, the death of Queen Victoria, took place during the war.
15. Beloved and famous British generals participated:
    (a) Lord Roberts, the hero of the Indian Campaigns was Commander-in-Chief in South Africa;
    (b) General Buller, the hero of the Zulu Wars, commanded the troops in Natal;
    (c) Lord Kitchener, the hero of the Sudan Campaign, was a general and later the Commander-in-Chief.

In Victorian England the population loved trinkets, tokens and curios. Every notable event was commemorated with the issue of a profusion of items, from silver statuettes of generals to Staffordshire figures, and from gold jewellery to celluloid lapel pins. This fad for commemoratives reached a peak during the celebrations of Queen Victoria's Diamond Jubilee in 1897 and from 1899 to 1902 during the Boer War. The countries in Europe in sympathy with the Boers reciprocated by issuing pro-Boer commemoratives and memorabilia.

This book will endeavour to give collectors an overview of the memorabilia that were issued in volume — items which became available to the general public and which today could be collected by the public. This book will not cover the field of 'militaria'. The collection of military items is a highly specialised field and cannot be covered in a few chapters.

The military service medals and military awards are well covered by some recently published books. This topic will therefore not be covered in this book.

For the general information of collectors, a chapter has been devoted to rare, one-of-a-kind commemoratives. These items are normally found in family collections, or in specialized collections or museums.

Books published during and after the Boer War cover a wide field and in this book reference is made only to those which have become highly collectible because of their illustrations, or have become good reference works on some field of commemoratives.

Readers may notice inaccuracies in the spelling of names or items in this book. The reason for this is that the names have been described exactly as they appear on the items.

Many of the items manufactured in Germany, Holland and France carry German, Dutch or French inscriptions, and these are recorded in the descriptions.

Readers will also notice that there are inconsistencies in the titles of many officers. The titles of officers did change during the course of the war: for example, at the beginning of the Boer War Baden-Powell was a Colonel; by its close he had risen in rank to Major-General.

The field of Boer War memorabilia is very diverse and not well documented. At regular intervals unknown and previously unrecorded items appear at the auction houses and in the antique stores and shops specialising in commemoratives. This book does not purport to cover the total field of Boer War collectibles, but I hope it will be a general guide for collectors. However, one of the great joys of collecting lies in the discovery of a rare or previously unknown or unrecorded item.

Pieter Oosthuizen
London.
1986

Chronological List of major Boer War events

31st May 1899	Bloemfontein Conference
8th September 1899	Britain sends 10,000 men to Natal
26th September 1899	Major-General Symons moves troops to Dundee
27th September 1899	President Kruger calls up burghers
7th October 1899	Lieutenant-General White lands at Durban
9th October 1899	President Kruger Ultimatum
11th October 1899	Outbreak of War
14th October 1899	Start of Siege of Kimberley
	Start of Siege of Mafeking
20th October 1899	Battle of Talana
21th October 1899	Battle of Elandslaagte
24th October 1899	Battle of Rietfontein
30th October 1899	Battle of Modderspruit
31st October 1899	General Buller lands at Cape Town
2nd November 1899	Start of Siege of Ladysmith
21st November 1899	Battle of Willow Grange
23rd November 1899	Battle of Belmont
25th November 1899	Battle of Graspan
26th November 1899	Battle of Derdepoort
28th November 1899	Battle of Modder River
10th December 1899	Battle of Stormberg
15th December 1899	Battle of Colenso
18th December 1899	Field Marshal Roberts appointed Commander-in-Chief
	General Kitchener appointed Chief of Staff
6th January 1900	Battle of Platrand (Wagon Hill)
10th January 1900	General Roberts lands at Cape Town
24th January 1900	Battle of Spion Kop

5th February 1900	Battle of Vaal Krantz
15th February 1900	Relief of Kimberley
18th February 1900	Battle of Paardeberg
27th February 1900	Surrender of General Cronje
28th February 1900	Relief of Ladysmith
7th March 1900	Battle of Poplar Grove
10th March 1900	Battle of Driefontein
13th March 1900	Capture of Bloemfontein
27th March 1900	Death of Commandant-General Joubert
31st March 1900	Battle of Sannah's Post
4th April 1900	Battle of Reddersburg
14th May 1900	Battle of Biggarsberg
17th May 1900	Relief of Mafeking
28th May 1900	Annexation of the Orange Free State
31st May 1900	Capture of Johannesburg
	Battle of Lindley
5th June 1900	Capture of Pretoria
7th June 1900	Battle of Roodewal
11th June 1900	Battle of Diamond Hill
12th June 1900	Capture of Volksrust
11th July 1900	Battle of Zilikaat's Nek
31st July 1900	Surrender of Commandant-General Prinsloo
27th August 1900	Battle of Bergendal (Dalmanutha)
6th September 1900	Capture of Lydenburg
19th October 1900	President Kruger sails for Europe
24th October 1900	General Buller sails for England
25th October 1900	Annexation of the Transvaal
6th November 1900	Battle of Bothaville
29th November 1900	General Kitchener appointed Commander-in-Chief
13th December 1900	Battle of Nooitgedacht
31st January 1901	Capture of Modderfontein
10th February 1901	Invasion of Cape Colony
28th February 1901	Middleburg Peace Talks
8th May 1901	High Commissioner Milner sails for England
17th September 1901	Battle of Blood River Poort
26th September 1901	Battle of Fort Itala
11th October 1901	Capture of Captain Scheepers
30th October 1901	Battle of Bakenlaagte
7th November 1901	Colonel Hamilton appointed Chief of Staff
16th December 1901	Capture of General Kritzinger
25th December 1901	Battle of Tweefontein
17th January 1902	Captain Scheepers executed
7th March 1902	Battle of Tweebosch
26th March 1902	Death of Cecil Rhodes
4th April 1902	Siege of Ookiep
11th April 1902	Battle of Rooiwal
12–18th April 1902	Peace Delegation meets in Pretoria
6th May 1902	Zulu attack on Holkrantz
15–18th May 1902	Boer Delegation meets in Vereeniging
31st May 1902	Peace Meeting in Vereeniging
	Peace Treaty signed in Pretoria

Alphabetical reference of names and places

A list of the most widely known and referred-to names and places

Aard, Frans: Boer commandant
Afrikaans: Boer language
Alleman's Nek, in the Drakensberg: action June 1900
Argyll and Sutherland Highlanders
Australian Bushmen
Australian Forces

Babington, Major-General J. M.
Babtie, Major Williams, V. C.
Baden-Powell, Major-General R. S. S.: CO Rhodesian Troopers
Badenhorst: Boer commandant
Bailey, Sir Abe: Rand mining magnate
Bakenlaagte, Transvaal: action October 1901
Balfour, A. J.: Deputy Prime Minister
Barnato, Barney: Rand mining magnate
Barton, Major-General Geoffrey: CO 6th Brigade
Bechuanaland Police Force
Bechuanaland Protectorate Regiment (Bechuanaland Rifles)
Belfast, Transvaal: action January 1901
Belfast Refugee Camp (concentration camp)
Belmont, Cape: action November 1900
Bergendal, Transvaal: action August 1901
Berkshire Regiment
Bester, A. J.: Boer commandant
Bethlehem Commando: Boer commando
Bethulie Commando: Boer commando
Bethune's Mounted Infantry
Bermuda prisoner-of-war camps
Beyers, Christiaan: Boer commandant
Blockhouse system
Bloemfontein: capital of the Orange Free State
Bloemfontein Refugee Camp (concentration camp)
Blood, General Bindon
Boksburg Commando: Boer commando
Border Mounted Rifles (Border Regiment)
Botha, Louis: Boer general
Botha, Philip: Boer general
Bothaville, Orange Free State: action November 1900

Brabant, Brigadier-General E. Y.
Brand, G. A.: Boer general
British South African Police
Britz: Boer commandant
Brandwater Basin, Orange Free State: action July 1900
Broadwood, Major-General R. G.: CO Cavalry Brigade
Brocklehurst, Colonel J. F.: CO Cavalry in Ladysmith
Broderick, St. John: Under-Secretary of War
Bruwer: Boer commandant
Buffelshoek, Transvaal: action December 1900
Buller, General Sir Redvers Henry, V. C.: CO 1st Army Corps
Bulwana Hill, Natal: action February 1900
Burger (Burgher), Schalk: acting Boer Commandant-General; Acting President of the Transvaal
Burmese Mounted Infantry
Burnham, Major Frederick Russel: American Chief of Scouts under Lord Roberts
Bushveldt Carbineers: Australian Anti-Commando Unit
Butler, Lieutenant-General Sir William: Acting Governor of the Cape Colony
Buys' Commando: Boer commando
Byng, Major J. H. G.: CO South African Light Horse

Cadet Corps in Mafeking: Forerunner of the Boy Scouts
Caesar's Camp, near Ladysmith, Natal: action January 1900
Cameron Highlanders (Cameronians)
Campbell, Major-General
Canadian Contingent
Canadian Scouts
Cape Dutch: Cape Boers or Boer language
Cape Mounted Rifles
Cape Police (South African forces)
Cape Rebels: Boer soldiers from the Cape
Cape Town: capital of the Cape Colony
Cape Town Highlanders
Carleton, Lieutenant-Colonel F. R. C.: CO Dublin Fusiliers
Caernarvon, Lord: Secretary for the Colonies
Carolina Commando: Boer commando
Carrington, General
Cecil, Major Lord Edward

Celliers: Boer commandant
Ceylon: prisoner-of-war camps
Ceylon Contingent
Chamberlain, Joseph: Secretary for the Colonies
Chermside, General
Cheshire Regiment
Chieveley, Natal: action December 1899
Chisholme, Colonel J. S.: CO Imperial Light Horse
Churchill, Winston: *Morning Post* correspondent
Churchill, Lady Randolph
Cilliers, J. G.: Boer general
City Imperial Volunteers (City of London Imperial Volunteers)
Clements, Major-General Ralph A. P.: CO 12th Brigade
Clery, Lieutenant General Sir Cornelius Francis: CO 2nd Infantry Division
Codrington, Lieutenant-Colonel Alfred F.: CO Coldstream Guards
Coke, Major-General John Talbot
Coldstream Guards
Colenbrander, General Johann: CO Kitchener's Fighting Scouts
Colenso, Natal: action December 1899
Colesburg, Cape Colony: action January 1900
Colley, Major-General Sir George P.: Commander at Majuba
Colonial Mounted Rifles
Colville, General Sir Henry: CO Ninth Division
Connaught Rangers
Conroy: Boer commandant
Consolidated Goldfields: Cecil Rhodes' company
Crofton, Lieutenant-Colonel Malby: CO Royal Lancaster Regiment
Cronje, Andries P.: Boer general
Cronje, Pieter Arnoldus ('Piet'): Boer general, leader of Transvaal forces on the Western Front
Cunningham, General

Dalgety, Colonel E. H.
Dalmanutha, Transvaal: action August 1901
Damant: Captain of Rimington's Tigers
Davies, Major W. D. ('Karri')
De Beers Diamond Corporation

Alphabetical reference of names and places xxi

De Jager: Boer commandant
De La Rey, Jacobus H. ('Koos'): Boer general
Derbyshire Regiment (Sherwood Foresters)
Derdepoort, Transvaal: place of action
De Villiers, C. J.: Boer commandant
Devonshire Regiment
De Vos: Boer commandant
De Wet, Christiaan: Boer general, guerilla leader
De Wet, Piet: Boer general
Dewetsdorp, Orange Free State: action November 1900
Diamond Field Horse Regiment
Diamond Hill, Transvaal: Action June 1900
Dick-Cunyngham, Lieutenant-Colonel W.: CO Gordon Highlanders
Diyatalawa: prisoner-of-war camp. Ceylon
Doornberg Commando: Boer commando
Doornkop, Transvaal: action May 1900
Dorsetshire Regiment
Douglas, General
Douthwaite Commando: Boer commando
Doyle, Dr Conan: author, doctor at Volunteer Hospital. Bloemfontein
Dragoon Guards
Drakensberg Mountain Range
Dublin Fusiliers
Duke of Cambridge's Own
Duke of Cornwall's Light Infantry
Duke of Edinburgh's Volunteer Rifles
Dundee, Natal: action October 1899
Dundonald, Colonel Earl of: CO Mounted Brigade
Dunlop, Lieutenant-Colonel J. W.: CO Royal Artillery Mounted Rifles
Du Plooy, Floris: Boer commandant
Durban, Natal: port of arrival of British troops
Durban Light Infantry
Durham Light Infantry
Du Toit: Boer general

Eastern Province Horse
East Kent Regiment (Buffs)
East Lancaster Regiment
East London Volunteers
East Surrey Regiment
East Yorkshire Regiment
Edward VII: King of England (Prince of Wales)

Edwards: Boer commandant
Elandsfontein, Transvaal: action May 1900
Elandslaagte, Natal: action October 1899
Elandsrivierpoort, Cape Colony: action September 1901
Elliot, Major-General E. Locke
Eloff, Sarel Johannes: Boer commandant
Emmett, Cheere: Boer commandant
Ennismore, Lord: Imperial Yeoman
Erasmus, Daniel: Boer commandant
Ermelo Commando: Boer commando
Essex Regiment
Ethelston, Commander R. N.: HMS *Powerful*

Fauresmith Commando: Boer commando
Ferreira, J. S.: Boer general
Ferreira, Pieter: Boer commandant
Ficksburg Commando: Boer commando
Fischer, Abraham: State Secretary of the Orange Free State
Fitzclarence, Captain Charles: CO Bechuanaland Protectorate Regiment
Fitzpatrick, Percy: Leader of the Uitlanders
Forestier-Walker, Lieutenant-General F. W.: GOC Cape
Fort Itala, Natal: action September 1901
Fouche, Willem: Boer commandant
Fourie, Piet: Boer general
Fouriesburg, Orange Free State: action July 1900
Frankfort Commando: Boer commando
Free State Commando: Boer commando
French, Major-General John D. P.: cavalry commander
French Commando: French mercenaries
Frere, Natal: action December 1899
Friend, The: newspaper
Froneman, C. C.: Boer general
Fuller, General J. F. C.

Gandhi, Mohandas Karamchand (Mahatma): Leader of the Stretcher Bearers with General Buller
Garratt, Lieutenant-Colonel F. S.: CO New Zealand Contingent
Gatacre, Lieutenant-General Sir William F.: CO 3rd Infantry Division
German Commando: German mercenaries
Gladstone, William Ewart: Liberal Leader
Gloucester Regiment
Gold mines, Transvaal

Gordon Highlanders
Gough, Lieutenant-Colonel Hubert de la P.: CO Mounted Infantry
Gough, Colonel George: CO 9th Lancers
Grant, General
Graspan, Cape Colony: action November 1899
Green Point, Cape Colony: prisoner-of-war camp
Grenadier Guards
Grenfell, Lieutenant-General
Griqualand Mounted Rifles
Grobler, H. S.: Boer commandant
Guards Brigade
Guerilla Commandos: Boer commandos
Guerilla warfare: Boer warfare (later stage of the war)
Gun Hill, Transvaal: action October 1901

Haasbroek (Hasebroek): Boer commandant
Haig, Major Douglas: Chief of Staff to General French and Lord Kitchener
Hamilton, Major-General Bruce: CO 21st Brigade
Hamilton, Colonel E. O. F.: CO Queen's Regiment
Hamilton, Colonel Ian (later Lieutenant-General) Chief of Staff to Lord Kitchener
Hampshire Regiment
Handy Men Guncrews of HMS *Powerful* and HMS *Terrible* who took Artillery overland to Ladysmith
Harrisburg Commando: Boer commando
Harrismith Commando: Boer commando
Hart, Major-General Arthur Fitzroy: CO Irish Brigade
Hart's Hill, Natal: action February 1900
Hassell's American Scouts
Hattingh: Boer general
Heidelberg Commando: Boer commando
Heidelberg Refugee Camp (concentration camp)
Heilbron, Orange Free State: action June 1900
Heilbron Commando: Boer commando
Hely-Hutchinson, Sir Walter: Governor of Natal
Heliographic Communications
Herzog (Hertzog), Judge James Barry: Boer general
Hertzog Commando: Boer commando

Hicks Beach, Sir Michael: Chancellor of the Exchequer
Highland Brigade
Highland Light Infantry
Highland Yeomanry
Hijs, P. L.: Boer commandant
Hilyard, Major-General H. J. T.: CO 2nd Brigade
Hlangwane Hill, Natal: action December 1899
Hobhouse, Emily: campaigner on concentration camps
Hofmeyr (Hofmeyer), Jan: Leader of Cape Afrikaners
Holkrantz, Transvaal: action May 1902
Hong Kong Contingent
Hore, Lieutenant-Colonel C.O.: CO Bechuanaland Protectorate Regiment
Household Cavalry (Composite Regiment)
Houtnek, Orange Free State: action May 1900
Hughes-Hallett, Lieutenant-Colonel J. W.: CO Seaforth Highlanders
Hunter, Major-General Sir Archibald: Chief of Staff to General Buller
Hussar Hill, Natal: action February 1900
Hussars (7th, 8th, 10th, 13th, 14th, 18th and 19th)
Hutton, General

Imperial Bushmen
Imperial Light Horse
Imperial Light Infantry
Imperial Yeomanry
India: prisoner-of-war camps
Inniskilling Fusiliers
Irish Brigade: Boer commando (Irish-American mercenaries)
Irish Fusiliers
Irish Rifles

Jacobsdal Commando: Boer commando
Jameson, Dr Leander Starr: Jameson Raid
Johannesburg, Transvaal: action May 1900
Johannesburg Commando: Boer commando
Johannesburg Contingent
Johannesburg Mounted Rifles
Johannesburg Police Commando (ZARPS): Boer commando
Johannesburg Refugee Camp (concentration camp)

Joubert, Petrus Jacobus ('Piet'): Boer general, CO Transvaal Forces

Kaffrarian Mounted Rifles
Keith-Falconer, Lieutenant-Colonel: CO Northumberland Fusiliers
Kekewich, Lieutenant-Colonel Robert G.: CO Loyal North Lancashire Regiment
Kelly-Kenny, Lieutenant-General Sir Thomas: CO 6th Infantry Division
Kemp, Christoffel Greyling: Boer general
Kimberley, Cape Colony: siege October 1899 to February 1900
Kimberley Light Horse
Kimberley Mounted Corps
Kimberley Refugee Camp (Concentration camp)
King's Own Scottish Borderers
King's Royal Rifle Corps
Kipling, Rudyard: *The Friend* correspondent
Kitchener of Khartoum, General Lord Horatio Herbert: Chief of Staff to Lord Roberts; later Commander-in-Chief
Kitchener, Colonel Frederick Walter: CO 5th Brigade, brother of Lord Kitchener
Kitchener's Bodyguard
Kitchener's Fighting Scouts
Klerksdorp, Transvaal: action March 1902
Knox, Major-General C. E.: CO 13th Brigade
Kock, Johannes Hermanus M.: Boer general
Kritizinger, Pieter Hendrik: Boer commandant-general
Kroonstad Commando: Boer commando
Kroonstad Refugee Camp (concentration camp)
Kruger, Stephanus Johannes Paulus ('Paul'): President of the South African Republic (Transvaal)
Krugersdorp Commando: Boer commando
Krupp: guns

Ladybrand Commando: Boer commando
Ladysmith, Natal: siege from November 1899 to February 1900
Laing's Nek, Natal: action June 1900
Lambert: Boer commandant
Lambton, Captain Hedworth R. N.: HMS *Powerful*
Lancashire Brigade
Lancashire Fusiliers
Lancashire Regiment
Lancaster Regiment
Lancers
Lang Riet, Orange Free State: action February 1902
Lansdowne, Marquis of: Secretary of State for War 1895–1900
Lategan: Boer commandant
Le Gallais, Lieutenant-Colonel P. W. J.: CO Mounted Infantry
Lee-Enfield: guns/rifles
Lee-Metford: guns/rifles
Leicester Regiment
Lemmer: Boer commandant
Leyds, Dr Willem: Foreign Secretary of the Transvaal
Lichtenburg Commando: Boer commando
Liebenberg: Boer commandant
Linchwe: Bechuana chief
Lincoln Regiment
Lindley, Orange Free State: action May 1900
Little, Lieutenant-Colonel M. O.: CO 9th Lancers
Liverpool Regiment
Long Toms: guns
Lotter, Johannes: Boer commandant
Louw: Boer commandant
Lovat's Scouts
Loyal North Lancashire Regiment
Lubbe: Boer commandant
Lumsden's Horse
Lydenburg Commando: Boer commando
Lyttelton, Major General Neville G.: CO 4th Brigade

Macbride, Major John: Commander of 'Irish Brigade' (Boer commando)
MacDonald, Major-General Sir Hector: CO Highland Brigade
Machadodorp, Transvaal: action July 1900
Machadodorp Commando: Boer commando
Mackinnon, Colonel W. H.
Mafeking, Cape Colony: siege from October 1899 to May 1900
Mafeking Town Guards
Magersfontein, Cape Colony: action December 1899
Mahon, Colonel Brian
Majuba: Battle of the First Boer War
Malan, Wynand: Boer commandant
Manchester Regiment

Mareuil Compte Georges Villebois de: Boer general
Maritz, Manie Solomon Gerhardus: Boer commandant
Marks, Samuel: friend of President Kruger
Marshall, General
Mauser: guns/rifles
Maxim machine guns
Maxwell, General John
Mears: Boer commandant
Merebank Refugee Camp (concentration camp)
Metcalfe, Lieutenant-Colonel C. T. E.: CO Rifle Brigade
Methuen, Lieutenant-General Lord Paul Sanford: CO 1st Infantry Division
Meyer, Lucas: Boer general
Middelburg Commando: Boer commando
Middlesex Regiment
Midland Mounted Rifles
Milner, Sir Alfred: High Commissioner for South Africa
Modder Rivier, Cape Colony: action November 1899
Moedwil, Transvaal: action September 1901
Möller, Lieutenant-Colonel Bernhard Drysdale: CO 18th Hussars
Montmorency's Scouts
Morant, Lieutenant 'Breaker': Bushveldt Carbineers (Australian Contingent)
Mounted Infantry
Munster Fusiliers
Muller, C. H.: Boer general
Myburgh: Boer commandant

Natal Artillery
Natal Carbineers
Natal Colony
Natal Mounted Rifles
Natal Royal Rifles
Natal Volunteers
National Scouts: Boers fighting with Britain
Naval Brigade
Naval Gun Hill, Natal: action December 1899
Nel: Boer commandant
New South Wales Bushmen
New South Wales Lancers
New Zealand Contingents
Nicholson's Nek, Natal: action October 1899
Nooitgedacht, Transvaal: action December 1900
Norcott, Major-General: CO 4th Brigade
Norfolk Regiment
Northamptonshire Regiment
North Lancashire Regiment
North Staffordshire Regiment
Northumberland Fusiliers
Norvals Point Refugee Camp (concentration camp)

Olifant's Nek, Transvaal: action August 1901
Olivier, Jan Hendrik: Boer general
Oosthuizen, Philip: Boer commandant
Oosthuizen, 'Red Bull': Boer field cornet
Opperman, Daniel: Boer commandant
Orange Free State, Boer Republic: later Orange River Colony
Orange Free State Commando: Boer commando
Orange River Colony
Oxfordshire Light Infantry

Paardeberg, Orange Free State: action February 1900
Paget, Major-General A. H.: CO 20th Brigade
Paget's Horse
Park, Lieutenant-Colonel
Pen-Symons, Major-General Sir William
Pepworth Hill, Natal: action October 1899
Phillips, Lieutenant L. March: Rimington's Tigers
Phipps-Hornby, Major Edmund: CO Royal Horse Artillery
Pienaar: Boer general
Pieter's Plateau, Natal: action February 1900
Piet Retief Commando: Boer commando
Pilcher, Colonel
Plumer, Lieutenant-Colonel Herbert: CO Rhodesian Mounted Infantry
Pole-Carew, Major-General R.: CO 9th Brigade
Poplar Grove, Orange Free State: action March 1900
Porter, Colonel T. C.
Potgieter, F. J.: Boer general
Powerful, HMS troopship
Pretoria: capital of the Transvaal
Pretoria Commando: Boer commando
Pretoria Mounted Police
Pretoria Refugee Camp (concentration camp)

Alphabetical reference of names and places xxv

Pretorius: Boer commandant
Pretyman, General Sir George
Prinsloo, Hendrik: Boer commandant
Prinsloo, Marthinus: General of the Orange Free State Forces
Prinsloo, Michael: Boer commandant: general
Protectorate Regiment

Queen's Regiment (West Surrey)
Queensland Contingent (Volunteers)
Queensland Mounted Infantry

Railway Pioneer Regiment
Ralph, Julian: *Daily Mail* war correspondent
Ramdam, Orange Free State: action February 1900
Rautenbach: Boer commandant
Reddersburg, Orange Free State: action April 1900
Reitz, Francis W.: State secretary of the Transvaal
Reitz, Orange Free State: action July 1901
Retief's Nek, Orange Free State: action July 1900
Rheeder: Boer commandant
Rhenoster Rivier, Orange Free State: action June 1900
Rhodes, Cecil John
Rhodesia
Rhodesian Regiment
Riddel, Lieutenant-Colonel H. E. Buchanan: CO 60th Rifles
Ridley, Colonel C. P.: CO Mounted Infantry
Rietfontein: action October 1899
Rifle Brigade
Rifles 60th
Rimington, Colonel: CO Royal Artillery Mounted Rifles
Rimington's Tigers: Guides or Scouts
Roberts, Field Marshall Lord Frederick Sleigh: Commander-in-Chief
Roberts, Lieutenant Hon. Frederick: son of Lord Roberts
Roch: Boer general
Roodewal, Orange Free State: action June 1900
Rooiwal, Transvaal: action April 1902
Ross, Captain Charles: Canadian Scouts
Ross: Boer commandant
Roux, Paul Hendrik: Boer general

Rouxville Commando: Boer commando
Royal Army Medical Corps
Royal Artillery Mounted Rifles
Royal Berkshire Regiment
Royal Canadian Dragoons
Royal Dragoons
Royal Engineers
Royal Fusiliers
Royal Highlanders (Black Watch)
Royal Horse Artillery Batteries
Royal Inniskilling Fusiliers
Royal Irish Regiment
Royal Irish Fusiliers
Royal Irish Rifles
Royal Lancaster Regiment
Royal Marines (Naval Brigade)
Royal Munster Fusiliers
Royal Scots Fusiliers
Royal Sussex Regiment
Royal Welsh Fusiliers
Royston, Colonel W.: CO colonial troops
Rundle, Lieutenant-General Sir Leslie: CO 8th and colonial divisions
Russian mercenaries
Rustenburg, Transvaal: action

St. Helena prisoner-of-war camps
Salisbury, Marquis: Prime Minister and Foreign Secretary 1895–1908
Sandspruit Refugee Camp (concentration camp)
Sannah's Post, Orange Free State: action March 1900
Scandinavian Corps: Boer commando
Scheepers, Captain Gideon: CO Boer Scout Corps
Schoeman: Boer general
Schreiner, William: Attorney-General of the Cape Colony
Schroder: Boer commandant (ZARPS)
Scots Fusiliers
Scots Greys
Scots Guards
Scott, Captain Percy M.: HMS *Terrible*
Scottish Borderers
Scottish Horse
Scottish Rifles (Cameronians)
Seaforth Highlanders
Senekal Commando: Boer commando
Shropshire Regiment (Light Infantry)
Sikh Contingent (Indian Forces)

Sim, Lieutenant-Colonel G. H.: CO Royal Engineers
Simonstown, Cape Colony: prisoner-of-war camp
Slabbert's Nek, Brandwater Basin: action
Smit, Nicolaas: Boer general
Smith-Dorrien, Major-General Horace A.: CO 19th Brigade
Smithfield Commando: Boer commando
Smuts, Jan C.: Transvaal State Attorney, Asistant Commandant-General
Smuts, Tobias: Boer general
Snyman, J. P.: Boer general
Somerset Light Infantry
South African Constabulary
South African Forces
South African Indian Ambulance Corps
South African Light Horse (Uitlanders)
South Australian Contingent
South Lancashire Regiment
South Wales Borderers
Spens, Colonel James: Shropshires
Spion Kop, Natal: action January 1900
Springfontein Refugee Camp (concentration camp)
Spruit: Boer commandant
Spytfontein Ridge: action
Staatsartillerie: Boer artillery
Standerton, Transvaal: action June 1901
Standerton Commando: Boer commando
Standerton Refugee Camp (concentration camp)
Steenkamp, Lucas: Boer commandant
Stephenson, Brigadier-General T. E.: CO 18th Brigade
Steyn: Boer commandant
Steyn, Marthinus Theunis: President of the Orange Free State Republic
Stormberg, Natal: action December 1899
Strathcona's Horse
Suffolk Mounted Infantry
Suffolk Regiment
Surprise Hill, Natal: action December 1899
Sussex Regiment
Swaziland Commando: Boer commando
Symons, Major-General Sir W. Penn: GOC Natal

Tabanyama Ridge, Natal: action January 1900
Talana Hill, Natal: action October 1899
Tasmanian Imperial Bushmen
Terrible, HMS: troop-ship
Thaba Nchu, Orange Free State: action
Thackeray, Lieutenant-Colonel T. M. G.: CO Inniskillings
Theron, Captain Danie: CO Boer Scout Corps
Theron, Sarel: Boer commandant
Theunissen: Boer commandant
Thorneycroft, Lieutenant-Colonel Alexander W.: CO Mounted infantry
Transvaal: South African Republic
Transvaal Colony
Trichardt, Piet: Boer commandant
Trichardt's Drift, Natal: action January 1900
Truter: Boer commandant
Tucker, Lieutenant-General Charles CO 7th Infantry Division
Tugela River: Natal
Tweebosch, Transvaal: action March 1902
Tweefontein: action December 1901

Uitlanders: foreigners in the Orange Free State and the Transvaal
Utrecht Commando: Boer commando
Uys: Boer commandant

Vaalkrans, Natal: action February 1900
Vaal River: between the Transvaal and Orange Free State
Van Coller: Boer commandant
Van der Merwe, Piet: Boer commandant
Van de Venter, Jacobus: Boer commandant
Van Niekerk, C. A.: Boer commandant
Van Zyl's Commando: Boer commando
Ventersburg, Orange Free State: action
Vereeniging, Transvaal: peace negotiations
Vermaas: Boer commandant
Victoria Mounted Rifles (Australian Forces)
Victoria, Queen
Viljoen, Ben: Boer commandant-general
Villebois-Mareuil, Georges Compte de: Boer general
Villiers, Colonel: CO South African Light Horse
Villonel: Boer commandant
Visser: Boer commandant
Vlakfontein, Transvaal: action May 1901
Von Donop, Lieutenant-Colonel Pelham
Vrede Commando: Boer Commando
Vryburg, Cape Colony: action

Vryheid Commando: Boer commando

Wagon Hill, Natal: action January 1900
Wakkerstroom Commando: Boer commando
Warren, Lieutenant-General Sir Charles: CO 5th Infantry Division
Warrenton Refugee Camp (concentration camp)
Warwickshire Regiment
Waterval Drift, Orange Free State: action February 1900
Waterval North Refugee Camp (concentration camp)
Wauchope, Major-General Andrew: CO Highland Brigade
Wavell, General
Weilbach: Boer commandant
Welsh Fusiliers
Welsh Regiment
Wepener, Orange Free State: action April 1900
Wernher, Beit & Co.: finance group
Wessels, C. J.: Boer general
Wessels, J. B.: Boer general
West Australian Mounted Infantry
West Kent Regiment
Weston, Major Hunter
West Riding Regiment
West Surrey Regiment
West Yorkshire Regiment

White, Lieutenant-General Sir George: GOC Natal
Willow Grange, Natal: action 1899
Wiltshire Regiment
Winburg Commando: Boer commando
Witwatersrand Gold Fields
Wolseley, Field Marshal Lord: Commander-in-chief of the Army in Britain
Wood, General Evelyn
Woodgate, Major-General E. R. P.: CO Lancashire Brigade
Wools-Sampson, Colonel Aubrey: CO Imperial Light Horse
Worcestershire Regiment
Wynne, General
York and Lancaster Regiment
Yorkshire Light Infantry
Yorkshire Regiment
Yule, Brigadier-General James H.: CO Infantry Brigade
Yzerspruit: action February 1902

Zand River, Orange Free State: action May 1900
ZARPS South African Republic Police Forces
Zilikaat's Nek: action July 1900
Zoutpansberg Commando: Boer commando
Zululand Colony
Zulus: the Zulu people

Boer War Victoria Cross Heroes

Albrecht, Herman: Trooper in Imperial Light Horse (Natal); action: Waggon Hill, Ladysmith, Natal, 6th January 1900

Atkinson, Alfred: Sergeant, 1st Battalion, The Yorkshire Regiment; action: Paardeberg, Orange Free State, 18th February 1900

Babtie, William: Major, Royal Army Medical Corps; action: Colenso, Natal, 15th December 1899

Barry, John: Private, 1st Battalion, The Royal Irish Regiment; action: Monument Hill, Belfast, Transvaal, 7–8th January 1901

Bees, William: Private, 1st Battalion, The Derbyshire Regiment; action: Moedwil, 30th September 1901

Beet, Harry Churchill: Corporal, 1st Battalion, The Nottingham and Derbyshire Regiment (Mounted Infantry); action Wakkerstroom, 22nd April 1900

Bell, Frederick William: Lieutenant, West Australian Mounted Infantry; action: Brakpan, Transvaal, 16th May 1901

Bisdee, John Hutton: Private, Tasmanian Imperial Bushmen; action: Warm Bad, Transvaal, 1st September 1900

Bradley, Frederick Henry: Driver, 69th Battery, Royal Field Artillery; action: Fort Itala, Natal, 26th September 1901

Brown, Edward Douglas: Major, 14th Hussars (The King's); action: Geluk, 13th October 1900

Buller, Sir Redvers Henry: General; was awarded the Victoria Cross while he served as Captain and Brevet Lieutenant-Colonel with 60th King's Rifles in Zululand during the Zulu war; action: Inhlobane Mountain, Zululand, 28th March 1879

Clements, John James: Corporal, Rimington's Guides; action: near Strijdenburg, 24th February 1900

Cockburn, Hampden Zane Churchill: Lieutenant, Royal Canadian Dragoons; action: Komati River, Transvaal, 7th November 1900

Congreve, Walter Norris: Captain, The 2nd Rifle Brigade (Prince Consort's Own); action: Colenso Bridge, Natal, 15th December 1899

Coulson, Gustavus Hamilton Blenkinsopp: Lieutenant, 1st Battalion, The King's Own Scottish Borderers; action: Lambrechtfontein, 18th May 1901

Crandon, Harry George: Private, 18th Hussars (Princess of Wales); action: Springboklaagte, 4th July 1901

Crean, Thomas Joseph: Surgeon-Captain, 1st

Imperial Light Horse; action: Tygerskloof, 18th December 1901

Cunyngham, William Henry Dick: Lieutenant-Colonel, The Gordon Highlanders; died Ladysmith, Natal, 6th January 1900; was awared the Victoria Cross while he served as Lieutenant, 2nd Battalion, The Gordon Highlanders at Sherpur Pass in Afghanistan, 13th December 1879

Curtis, Albert Edward: Private, 2nd Battalion, The East Surrey Regiment; action: Onderbank Spruit, 23rd February 1900

Douglas, Henry Edward Manning: Lieutenant, Royal Army Medical Corps; action: Magersfontein, 11th December 1899

Doxat, Alexis Charles: Lieutenant, 3rd Battalion, Imperial Yeomanry; action: Zeerust, 20th October 1900

Dugdale, Frederic Brooks: Lieutenant, 5th Royal Irish Lancers; action: near Derby, 3rd March 1901

Durrant, Alfred Edward: Private, 2nd Battalion, The Rifle Brigade (Prince Consort's Own); action: Bergendal, 27th August 1900

Engleheart, Henry William: Sergeant, 10th Hussars (Prince of Wales' Own Royal); action: north of Bloemfontein, Orange Free State, 13th March 1900

English, William John: Lieutenant, 2nd Scottish Horse; action: Vlakfontein, 3rd July 1901

Farmer, Donald Dickson: Sergeant, 1st Battalion, The Queen's Own Cameron Highlanders; action: Nooitgedacht, 13th December 1900

Firth, W.: Sergeant, 1st Battalion, The Duke of Wellington's West Riding Regiment; action: Plewman's Farm, near Arundel, Cape Colony, 24th February 1900

Fitzclarence, Charles: Captain, The Royal Fusiliers; action: Siege of Mafeking, 14th–27th October and 26th December 1899

Glasock, Horace Henry: Driver, 'Q' Battery, Royal Horse Artillery; action: Korn Spruit, Modder River, Orange Free State, 31st March 1900

Gordon, William Eagleson: Captain, 1st Battalion, The Gordon Highlanders; action: Doornboschfontein (Leehoehoek), 11th July 1900

Hampton, Harry: Sergeant, 1st Battalion, The King's Liverpool Regiment; action: Van Wyk's Vlei, 21st August 1900

Hardham, William James: Farrier-Sergeant-Major, 4th New Zealand Contingent; action: during 'guerilla' warfare on 28th January 1901

Heaton, William Edward: Private, 1st Battalion, The King's Liverpool Regiment; action: Geluk, 23rd August 1900

Holland, Edward James Gibson: Sergeant, Royal Canadian Dragoons; action: Komati River, Transvaal, 7th November 1900

House, William: Private, 2nd Battalion, The Royal Berkshire Regiment, action: Mosilikaats Nek, 2nd August 1900

Howse, Neville Reginald: Captain, New South Wales Medical Staff Corps (Australian Forces); action: Vredefort, 24th July 1900

Ind, Alfred Ernest: Shoeing Smith, Royal Horse Artillery; action: Tafelkop, Orange River Colony, 20th December 1901

Inkson, Edgar Thomas: Lieutenant, Royal Army Medical Corps, attending the Royal Inniskilling Fusiliers; action: Hart's Hill, Colenso, Natal, 24th February 1900

Johnston, Robert: Captain, Imperial Light Horse (Natal); action: Elandslaagte, 21st October 1899

Jones, Robert James Thomas Digby: Lieutenant, Royal Engineers; action: Ladysmith, Natal, 6th January 1900

Kennedy, Charles Thomas: Private, 1st Battalion, The Highland Light Infantry; action: Dewetsdorp, 22nd November 1900

Kirby, Frank Howard: Corporal, Royal Engineers; action: by Delagoa Bay Railway in the Transvaal, 2nd June 1900

Knight, Henry James: Corporal, 1st Battalion, The King's Liverpool Regiment; action: Van Wyk's Vlei, 21st August 1900

Lawrence, Brian Turner Tom: Sergeant, 17th Lancers; action: patrol duty, 7th August 1900

Le Quesne, Ferdinand Simeon: Surgeon, Royal Army Medical Corps; was awarded the Victoria Cross while he served as Surgeon with the medical staff at the Village of Tartan in Burma, 4th May 1889

Lodge, Isaac: Gunner, 'Q' Battery, Royal Horse Artillery; action: Korn Spruit, Modder River, Orange Free State, 31st March 1900

Mackay, John Frederick: Lance-Corporal, 1st Battalion, The Gordon Highlanders; action: Crow's Nest Hill, near Johannesburg, Transvaal, 29th May 1900

Mansel-Jones, Conwyn: Captain, The West Yorkshire Regiment; action: Terrace Hill, north of Tugela, Natal, 27th February 1900

Marling, Percival Scrope: Colonel, 18th Hussars; was awarded the Victoria Cross while he served as Lieutenant, 3rd Battalion, The King's Royal Rifle Corps, at the Battle of Tamaai, Sudan, 13th March 1884

Martineau, Horace Robert: Sergeant, Protectorate Regiment (N. W. Cape Colony); action: defence of Mafeking at Game Tree, 26th December 1899

Martin-Leake, Arthur: Surgeon-Captain, South African Constabulary; action: Vlakfontein, 8th February 1902

Masterson, James Edward Ignatius: Lieutenant, 1st Battalion, The Devonshire Regiment; action: Waggon Hill (Platrand) Natal, 6th January 1900

Maxwell, Francis Aylmer: Lieutenant, Indian Staff Corps, attached to Roberts' Light Horse; action: Korn Spruit, Modder River, Orange Free State, 31st March 1900

Maygar, Leslie Cecil: Lieutenant, 5th Victoria Mounted Rifles (Australian Forces); action: Geelhoutboom, 23rd November 1901

Meiklejohn, Matthew Fontaine Maury: Captain, 2nd Battalion, The Gordon Highlanders; action: Elandslaagte, 21st October 1899

Milbanke, Sir John Peniston: Lieutenant, 10th Hussars (Prince of Wales' Own Royal); action: Colesberg. 5th January 1900

Mullins, Charles Herbert: Captain Light Imperial Horse (Natal); action: Elandslaagte, 21st October 1899

Nickerson, William Henry Snyder: Lieutenant, Royal Army Medical Corps, attached to Mounted Infantry; action: Wakkerstroom, 20th April 1900

Norwood, John: Second Lieutenant, 5th Dragoon Guards (Princess Charlotte of Wales'); action: Ladysmith, 30th October 1899

Nurse, George Edward: Corporal, 66th Battery, Royal Field Artillery; action: Colenso Bridge, Natal, 15th December 1899

Parker, Charles Edward Haydon: Sergeant, 'Q' Battery, Royal Horse Artillery; action: Korn Spruit/Modder River, Orange Free State, 31st March 1900

Parsons, Francis Newton: Lieutenant, 44th Essex Regiment; action: Paardeberg, 18th February 1900; died: Driefontein, 10th March 1900

Phipps-Hornby, Edmund John: Major, 'Q' Battery, Royal Horse Artillery; action: Modder River, Orange Free State, 31st March 1900

Pitts, James: Private, 1st Battalion, The Manchester Regiment; action: Caesar's Camp, Natal (Ladysmith), 6th January 1900

Price-Davies, Llewellyn Alberic Emilius: Lieutenant, The King's Royal Rifle Corps; action: Blood River Poort, 17th September 1901

Ramsden, Horace Edward: Trooper, Protectorate Regiment (N. W. Cape Colony); action: Game Tree, Mafeking, 26th December 1899

Ravenhill, George: Private, 2nd Battalion, The Royal Scots Fusiliers; action: Colenso, Natal, 15th December 1899

Reed, Hamilton Lyster: Captain, 7th Battery, Royal Field Artillery; action: Colenso, Natal, 15th December 1899

Richardson, Arthur Herbert Lindsay: Sergeant, Lord Strathcona's Horse (Canadian Forces); action: Wolvespruit, north of Standerton, 5th July 1900

Roberts, The Hon. Frederick Hugh Sherston: Lieutenant, The King's Royal Rifle Corps; action: Colenso, Natal, 15th December 1899; died: Chieveley, Natal, 17th December 1899

Roberts, Lord Frederick Sleigh: Commander-in-Chief; was awarded the Victoria Cross while he served as Lieutenant in Bengal Artillery at Khodagunge in India, 2nd January 1858

Robertson, William: Sergeant-Major, 2nd Battalion, The Gordon Highlanders; action: Elandslaagte, 21st October 1899

Rogers, James: Sergeant, South African Constabulary; action: near Thaba'Nchu, Orange Free State, 15th June 1901

Schofield, Harry Norton: Captain, Royal Field Artillery; action: Colenso Bridge, Natal, 15th December 1899

Scott, Robert: Private, 1st Battalion, The Manchester Regiment; action: Caesar's Camp, Ladysmith, Natal, 6th January 1900

Shaul, John David Francis: Corporal, 1st Battalion, The Highland Light Infantry; action: Magersfontein, 11th December 1899

Towse, Ernest Beechcroft Beckwith: Captain, 1st Battalion, The Gordon Highlanders, action: Magersfontein, 11th December 1899; action: Mount Theba, 30th April 1900

Traynor, William Bernard: Sergeant, 2nd Battalion, The West Yorkshire Regiment; action: Bothwell Camp, 6th February 1901

Turner, Richard Ernest William: Lieutenant, Royal Canadian Dragoons; action: Komati River, Transvaal, 7th November 1900

Ward, Charles: Private, 2nd Battalion, The King's Own Yorkshire Light Infantry; action: Lindley, 26th June 1900; last awardee decorated by Queen Victoria before her death

Wylly, Guy George Egerton: Lieutenant, Tasmanian Imperial Bushmen; action: Warm Bad, Transvaal, 1st September 1900

Young, Alexander: Sergeant-Major, Cape Police (South African Forces); action: Ruiter's Kraal, 13th August 1901

Younger, David Reginald: Captain, 1st Battalion, The Gordon Highlanders; action: Doornboschfontein (Leehoehoek), Transvaal, 11th July 1900

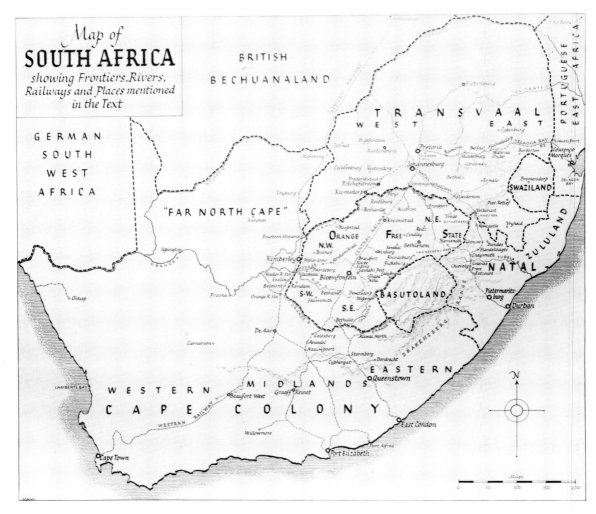

Map of South Africa (1900)

BOER WAR MEMORABILIA

CHAPTER 1

General Ceramics

Plates, services, tea-sets, loving cups, mugs, tumblers, tobacco jars and general items

Today ceramics are still very popular with collectors, and there is hardly a home where some prized ceramic piece is not on display.

At the end of the nineteenth century ceramic products — both porcelain (hard paste) and pottery (soft paste) — were the most popular medium used by the manufacturers of memorabilia. It was relatively cheap for the manufacturers of porcelain and pottery to manufacture these items in bulk. A representation of a Boer War event, a particular emblem, or a portrait of a general was normally transfer-printed on the ware.

The range of Boer War ceramics was very wide, extending from plates produced for stores as 'give-aways' at one extreme to the highly prized and expensive Worcester porcelain figures at the other. Every major battle or event was remembered or celebrated with a range of ceramics honouring the generals involved. Very often a whole tea or dinner service was produced decorated with one emblem, event or general. Collectors will find that the same decoration was used on a great number of different items.

Many of these items were in daily use in homes and even, if they have survived, show a lot of wear. Other items were treasured and carefully displayed by their owners and are still in very good condition.

While most of the pro-British ceramics were produced in the United Kingdom, almost all the pro-Boer ceramics were produced in European countries.

Plate 1
A Copeland porcelain loving cup made for T. Goode & Co., South Audley St., London (subscribers' copies).
Side 1: '1899 Transvaal War 1900'.
A medallion with picture of Queen Victoria and the wording 'Victoria Queen and Empress — Comforter of the Afflicted' surrounded with the Empire flags and the emblems of the Colonies.
'Equal rights for all'.

Side 2: 'Imperial Federation'.
Four circles with pictures and a listing of the

major events of the war up to this period. 'Unity is strength'.

Side 3: 'Britannia Tower of Justice'. Medallion with a picture of Britannia and a miner flanked by an Imperial Volunteer and a Royal Marine.
'Defender of the Oppressed'.
Inside the rim: a list of the key commanding officers. (5½ in. – 14 cm.)
(From the Oosthuizen Collection)

Plate 2
A Doulton Lambeth blue glaze loving cup with a silver rim. On the front a medallion picture of Queen Victoria flanked by Empire flags with the inscription: 'In Commemoration of the hoisting of the British flag at Pretoria' and 'God save the Queen'.
(6¾ in. – 17.1 cm.)
(From the Oosthuizen Collection)

Plate 3

Figure 1: A Doulton brown glaze eathenware jug with a picture of a wounded Royal Marine with the inscription 'The Handy Man' flanked by pictures of 'Capt H. Lambton' and 'Capt P. M. Scott'.
Impressed Doulton, Lambeth, England.
$(8\frac{1}{2}$ in. – 21 cm.)
(*From the Oosthuizen Collection*)

Figure 2: A Doulton brown glaze earthenware jug decorated with an oval print of Lord Roberts, flanked by British flags and a lion, kangaroo, ostrich and beaver. The sides with oval pictures of Colonel Baden-Powell and Major-General French with the inscription 'South Africa 1900'.
Impressed Doulton, Lambeth, England.
$(8\frac{1}{4}$ in. – 21 cm)
(*From the Oosthuizen Collection*)

Plate 4

A large Doulton loving cup with a medallion picture of Queen Victoria backed by two crossed flags. The rest of the cup is decorated with roses, thistles and clover. Above the medallion is the wording 'In commemoration of the hoisting of the flag at Pretoria' and below the medallion the wording 'God save the Queen'.
Maker's impression: Doulton, Lambeth, England 9962.
(Height $10\frac{1}{4}$ in. – 26 cm.)
(*From the Oosthuizen Collection*)

Plate 5

A Doulton blue glaze earthenware jug decorated with an oval medallion with Queen Victoria flanked by flags of the British Empire with the inscription 'In commemoration of the hoisting of the flag at Pretoria'.
Impressed Doulton, Lambeth.
$(8\frac{1}{4}$ in. – 21 cm.)
(*From the Oosthuizen Collection*)

Plate 6

Vases and jugs in various sizes were made by 'Elliott, London' to commemorate the Relief of Mafeking.

Figure 1: A small jug with the inscription:
'Mafeking Relieved'
'God save the Queen and bless B.P.'
'This little pot was made a few hours after Colonel Mahon marched into Mafeking on Thursday morning May 17th 1900'.
$(3\frac{3}{4}$ in. – 9.5 cm.)

Boer War Memorabilia

Plate 7

Figure 1: A multicolour porcelain cup. On the green and gold border around the rim the wording 'Equal rights for all'. Around the cup pictures of 'Field Marshal Lord Roberts — Commander in Chief of our Forces in South Africa', Queen Victoria, and leading generals.
On the base the emblems and the names of the participating Colonies: Canada, Natal, India, New South Wales, Tasmania, Victoria, New Zealand, Queensland and Cape Colony.
On the inside of the rim the names of the key generals and Boer War battles.
Impressed: Copeland Late Spode. Rd. 180288 England. (6 in. – 15.2 cm.)

Figure 2: A green glaze jug with the face of a soldier and a marine. On the cap of the marine the inscription 'HMS Terrible' and on the rim of the base 'Our navy' and 'Our army'.
On the base: England Rd. 406.932.
($5\frac{1}{2}$ in. – 14 cm.)

Figure 3: A jug with the wording 'Surrender of Cronje to Lord Roberts' under the picture. Unmarked. (6 in. – 15.2 cm.)
(*All from the collection of Mr Kenneth Griffith, London*)

Figure 2 : A jug with a dog handle (on the dog's collar the name 'Creaky') with the inscription:
'The heroic defender of Mafeking'
The raised letters 'B.P.'
'Sit tight and shoot straight'
'Telegram from Colonel Baden-Powell — October 21st 1899. All well — Four hours bombardment — one dog killed'
'Here he is on the handle'
'Telegram from Mafeking April 20th — We can stick it out for two months or more — All well — Nobody minds'
Mafeking Relieved May 17th 1900'
'God save the Queen'.
(7 in. – 17.8 cm.)
(*Both from the Oosthuizen Collection*)

General Ceramics

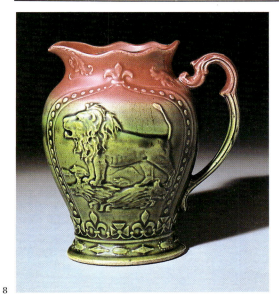

Plate 8
A red and green glaze jug with an imperial lion standing on boars (Boers) with the crossed flags and crown on the back.
This jug was also produced in different colours.
Impressed on the bottom: 1901 Patent Office Registration Number. ($6\frac{1}{4}$ in. – 15.9 cm.)
(*From the Oosthuizen Collection*)

Plate 9
White plates with open-work borders. Many different kinds of open-work border plates were produced and each of the manufacturers issued a series with the pictures of the Boer War generals.

Figure 1: Plate with 'Lord Roberts'.
Unmarked. ($8\frac{1}{4}$ in. – 21 cm.)

Figure 2: Plate with 'General Sir Redvers Buller'.
Marked: Knight Aldershot.
($8\frac{5}{8}$ in. – 21.9 cm.)
(*Both from the Oosthuizen Collection*)

Plate 10
Different plates were produced, all with the same transfer print with a picture of 'Field Marshal Lord Roberts V.C.' in a medallion. Some of the pictures have wording around them or a sprig or laurel added.

Figure 1: With the wording 'Always to the Front!'. ($8\frac{5}{8}$ in. 21.9 cm.)

Figure 2: With a laurel branch.
($8\frac{1}{2}$ in. – 21.6 cm.)

Figure 3: Only with the medallion.
(8¼ in. – 22.2 cm.)
(*From the Oosthuizen Collection*)

Plate 11
A plate with a blue glaze border with the figures of an Imperial Volunteer and a Highlander shaking hands above an inaccurate Victoria Cross with the inscription: 'Sons of the Empire'.
Maker's mark: Glasgow Fleming Britain.
(10 in. – 25.3 cm.)
(*By courtesy of Rita & Ian Smythe, Britannia, London*)

Plate 12
Figure 1: A small plate with a picture of General Buller, two crossed flags and the wording: 'General Sir Redvers Buller V C'. One of a series with different generals.
Maker's mark: 'Registered Chapman England'. (6¼ in. – 15.9 cm.)

Figure 2: Plate with medallion pictures of 'Lord Kitchener', 'Sir Redvers Buller' and

'Lord Roberts' flanked by two soldiers. Maker's mark: W & R Stoke on Trent Carlton Ware (Wiltshaw & Robinson Ltd.). (6¾ in. – 17 cm.)

Figure 3: A plate with a picture of Lord Roberts and two crossed flags and the wording: 'Bobs!', 'Our Bobs!' and 'Field Marshal Lord Roberts'.
Maker's mark: C. Hadman. By permission of 'Black & White' Russell & Sons.
(7 in. – 17.7 cm.)
(*All from the Oosthuizen Collection*)

Plate 13
A plate with a photograph picture with the wording 'Baden-Powell'.
(*By permission of the National Army Museum, London*)

Plate 14
A series of white plates were issued with the pictures of Boer War generals.

Figure 1: With picture of 'Field Marshal Lord Roberts'.

Figure 2: With picture of 'Lieut. General French'.

13

14

15

Figure 3: With picture of 'General Hector MacDonald C.B.'.
Unmarked (8 in. – 20.3 cm.)
(*From the Oosthuizen Collection*)

Plate 15

Figure 1: A plate with a glazed terracotta border with a picture and the wording: 'Lieut-General French'.
One of a series with pictures of various generals. (9¾ in. – 24.7 cm.)

Figure 2: With picture of 'Lord Kitchener'.

Figure 3: With picture of 'Lord Roberts'.
Two plates of a series with brown glazed borders. (9¾ in. – 24.7 cm.)
(*All from the Oosthuizen Collection*)

Plate 16

A Coalport plate with blue transfer printing on a white plate. Also made with a gold border and with blue transfer printing on a gold backround.
On the front: A picture of Lord Roberts in a Medal with the names of all the key battles and generals.
On the back the wording:
'South African War — Field Marshall Lord Roberts V.C. & C and his principal Commanding Officers — Boer Ultimatum 10th Oct. 1899
Orange River Colony Vaal River Colony Late Orange Free State Late S.A. Republic Annexed 27th May 1900 Annexed 1st Sept. 1900'. (10½ in. – 26.6 cm.)
(*From the Oosthuizen Collection*)

Plate 17

Figure 1: A plate with a medallion flanked by a Highlander and a Colonial Trooper and two crossed Empire Flags with the following inscriptions:
'Freedom Liberty Equality'
'Ready — Aye — Ready'
'War declared in South Africa by President Kruger Oct 11th 1899'
'Lord Roberts Commander in Chief of Cape Colony'
'General Buller Commander in Chief of Natal'
'God save our Queen'
'Britannia mourns her Heroes now at rest'

'England expects every man to do his duty'.
(9½ in. – 24.1 cm.)

Figure 2: A small square plate with fluted border, with a medallion consisting of two crossed flags flanked by a Highlander and a Lancer with the following wording:
'Naval Brigade'
'Ready — Aye — Ready'
'Each doing his Country's work'
'1899 – 1900'. (5 in. – 12.7 cm.)

Figure 3: A plate with a portrait picture of 'Lord Roberts' in the centre and surrrounded by decorations.

First: a medallion with Baden-Powell flanked by flags with the wording:
'Maj. General Baden-Powell Defender of Mafeking' and 'Either conquer or die'.

Second: a medallion flanked by soldiers with flags of the Royal Navy and Royal Marine and the wording: 'The Handy Man' and 'Soldiers of the Queen'.

Third: pictures of 'Sir George White' and 'Sir Redvers Buller' flanked by flags with the wording: 'Defender and Reliever of Ladysmith' and 'By valour steadfastness'.

Fourth: a medallion consisting of flags flanked by a Canadian Artillery man and New South Wales Lancer with the wording: 'Soldiers of the Queen'.
All unmarked. (9½ in. – 24.1 cm.)
(*All from the Oosthuizen Collection*)

Plate 18

Figure 1: A small plate with soldiers around a cannon with the wording: 'Christmas 1900' and 'A present from William Bros'.
Unmarked. (8½ in. – 21.6 cm.)

Figure 2: A scalloped plate with five medallion pictures of generals flanked by flags: 'Gen Buller', 'Gen Lord Kitchener', 'Lord Roberts', 'Gen Sir Geo White' and 'Gen Hector MacDonald'.
Maker's mark: D L & S Our Heroes (David Lockhart & Sons).
(10 $\frac{1}{8}$ in. – 25.7 cm.)

Figure 3: One of a series of plates with generals with green glazed borders, with a photographic picture of 'Lord Roberts'.
Unmarked (8¾ in. – 22.2 cm.)
(*All from the Oosthuizen Collection*)

Plate 19
Two gold-rimmed plates with battle scenes in the centre transfer-printed in brown and black with the wording: 'Our Boys at the Front' and 'For Queen and Country'.

Figure 1: With brown centre.

Figure 2: With black centre.
The plates were also produced without the gold rim.
Unmarked. (8¾ in. – 22.2 cm.)
(*From the Oosthuizen Collection*)

10 Boer War Memorabilia

19

Plate 20
A series of square green glaze bordered wall plaques were manufactured with pictures of the generals.

Figure 1: With the picture of Lord Kitchener and the wording: 'The Sirdar'.

Figure 2: With the picture of 'General Sir W. F. Gateacre'.
Unmarked. $(7\frac{1}{2} \times 8\frac{1}{4}$ in. $- 19 \times 21$ cm.)
(*From the Oosthuizen Collection*)

Plate 21
Figure 1: One of a series of glazed tiles with pictures of generals, with the picture of 'General Sir Redvers Buller V.C.'.
Marked: England. $(6 \times 6$ in. $- 15 \times 15$ cm.)
Figure 2: One of a series of round wall plaques with pictures of the generals. They were also used as teapot stands. This one with the picture of 'General Sir Redvers H. Buller V.C. G.C.B. K.C.M.G. P.C.'.
Unmarked. $(6\frac{1}{2}$ in. $- 16.5$ cm.)
(*Both from the Oosthuizen Collection*)

20

General Ceramics 11

21

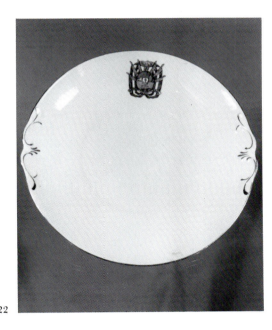

22

23

Plate 22
A porcelain plate with the coat-of-arms of the South African Republic.
Maker's mark: Royal Vale China, H. J. C. Longton England. (8 in. – 20.3 cm.)
(*By courtesy of the National Cultural History and Open-Air Museum, Pretoria*)

Plate 23
A lustre ware tea stand with Lady Peace standing over British and Boer soldiers shaking hands. The picture is flanked with the names of generals: 'Roberts, Kitchener, French, White, B. P.' and 'Joubert, Botha, De Wet, Delarey, Villiers'.
The peace picture carries the following words: 'Peace and Prosperity', 'Unity is Strength' and 'Peace Proclaimed Sunday June 1st 1902'.
(5 in. – 12.7 cm.)
(*By courtesy of the National Cultural History and Open-Air Museum, Pretoria*)

Plate 24
Part of a service made by the Florentine China company in England with the coat-of-arms of the Orange Free State Republic.
(*By courtesy of the National Cultural History and Open-Air Museum, Pretoria*)

Plate 26
A large terracotta plaque of General Sir Redvers Buller made by A. George.
$(15\frac{1}{2} \times 12\frac{1}{4}$ in. $- 39.3 \times 31.1$ cm.$)$
(*From the collection of Mr Kenneth Griffith, London*)

Plate 27

Figure 1: A mug with a round picture of Queen Victoria surrounded by the words: 'War in South Africa'. 'Transvaal Colony', 'Orange River Colony' and 'Added to the Empire 1900'.

Plate 25
A lustre ware plaque with a blue glaze border and a brown glaze inner rim with a British soldier and a Boer shaking hands in front of Lady Peace with the wording:'Peace and Prosperity' and 'Unity is Strength'.
Below the picture the words: 'Peace proclaimed Sunday June 1st 1902'.
Unmarked. $(12 \times 11$ in. $- 30.5 \times 28$ cm.$)$
(*From the collection of Mr Kenneth Griffith, London*)

General Ceramics

On the back: 'St. Buryan Cornwall'.
Unmarked. (4⅞ in. – 9.9 cm.)

Figure 2: A pottery match holder with a round picture of 'Lord Roberts' flanked by two flags and two soldiers.
On the back pictures of Lord Kitchener and Sir Redvers Buller.
Maker's mark: W & R Stoke on Trent Carlton Ware (Wiltshaw & Robinson Ltd.).
(2½ in. – 6.3 cm.)

Figure 3: A mug with a brown transfer print of an Imperial Lion surrounded by flags. Around the rim the wording: 'South Africa 1899–1900' and on either side of the lion 'Union is Strength' and 'Peace with honour'.
Maker's mark: J. G. & N. London.
(3⅛ in. – 8 cm.)

(*All from the Oosthuizen Collection*)

Plate 28

One of a series of mugs with pictures of generals. This one with the picture of 'Lieut-General Sir George White V.C. G.C.B.'.
Unmarked.
(*By permission of the National Army Museum, London*)

Plate 29

A brown Derbyware mug, signed by T. H. Taylor with the inscription: 'Ladysmith relieved Feb 28th 1900 Gen. Buller'.
(*By permission of the National Army Museum, London*)

Plate 30

Figure 1: A brown glaze character jug of President Kruger.
Unmarked. (7 in. – 17.8 cm.)

Figure 2: A brown glaze whisky jug with a silver top and a medallion with the picture of Colonel Baden-Powell.
Maker's mark: Taylor, Tunnicliffe & Co. Ltd., Hanly. (6½ in. – 16.5 cm.)
(*By courtesy of Rita & Ian Smythe, Britannia, London*)

Plate 31
A portrait jug of Lord Kitchener.
(*In the collection of Major Philip Erskine, Stellenbosch*)

Plate 32
Two small porcelain vases marked '297' with Boer War scenes.

Figure 1: Empire soldiers around a mounted soldier.

Figure 2: Empire soldiers around a cannon.
(6⅜ in. – 16.2 cm.)
(*From the Oosthuizen Collection*)

General Ceramics

Plate 33

Figure 1: A small fluted porcelain tumbler with a picture of 'Major-General Baden-Powell' and the wording: 'The Pillar of a People's Hope'.
On the back: 'In Commemoration of the Glorious Defense & Relief of Mafeking' and 'Siege commenced Oct 14th 1899 Relief effected May 17th 1900'.
Maker's mark: The Foley China.
($3\frac{1}{4}$ in. – 8.3 cm.)

Figure 2: A cup and saucer with a medal with a picture of Lord Roberts flanked by two soldiers with the words: 'The Army', 'Colonies — Supporters of the Empire — Volunteers'. Also a wreath with the following names: 'Roberts — Buller — Kitchener — White — Baden-Powell — French'.
On the inside of the rim of the cup in a banner the words: 'An Empire founded on Liberty'.
(Saucer: $5\frac{1}{2}$ in. – 14 cm.; cup $2\frac{1}{2}$ in. – 6.3 cm.)
Maker's mark: The Foley China England Rd. 354781.
This design was also used on tea-sets and dinner services.

Figure 3: A porcelain cup and saucer. The cup has pictures of 'Sir George White' and 'Sir Redvers Buller' flanked by flags and the words: 'Defender and Reliever of Ladysmith' and 'By Valour & Steadfastness'.
In the saucer a picture of 'Lord Roberts Commander in Chief South Africa' flanked by flags and the wording: 'Heavens Light our Guide' and 'Virtute Valore'.
Unmarked.
(Saucer $6\frac{1}{4}$ in. – 15.9 cm.; cup $3\frac{1}{4}$ in. – 8.3 cm.)

Figure 4: A fluted cup and saucer with decorations similar to Figure 2.
(Saucer $5\frac{3}{4}$ in. – 14.6 cm.; cup $2\frac{1}{4}$ in. – 5.7 cm.)
Maker's mark: The Foley China England Rd. 116610.

(*All from the Oosthuizen Collection*)

34

Plate 34

Figure 1: A tumbler with the 'Peace' picture with the words: 'Peace and Prosperity' and 'Unity is Strength'.
Unmarked. ($4\frac{1}{2}$ in. – 10.8 cm.)

Figure 2: A milk jug with a picture of 'Field Marshal Lord Roberts V.C.'.
Unmarked. ($4\frac{1}{8}$ in. – 10.5 cm.)

Figure 3: A mug with a Handy man and a soldier flanking the Emblem and the wording: '1899–1900 South Africa'.
Unmarked. ($3\frac{2}{5}$ in. – 8.3 cm.)

Figure 4: A porcelain tumbler with a picture of 'Lord Roberts' flanked by two sets of crossed flags.
On the back: 'Peace Rejoicing — 1900 — Radcliffe on Trent'.
Maker's mark: W & Sons Rd. 205542.
($3\frac{5}{8}$ in. – 9.2 cm.)

Figure 5: A porcelain mug with pictures of King Edward VII and Queen Alexandra flanked by flags and the words: 'God bless them', 'Crowned June 26th 1902' and 'Enthoned in the Hearts of their People'.
On the back the 'Peace' picture of the Boer War.
Maker's mark: Stoke-on-Trent, Trade Bros Mark, Staffordshire, England A.
($3\frac{1}{4}$ in. – 8.2 cm.)

Figure 6: A milk jug with a picture of a Marine — on his hat band 'H.M.S. Powerful' and under his picture 'The Handy Man'.
Unmarked. ($4\frac{1}{8}$ in. – 10.5 cm.)

Figure 7: A mug with soldiers flanking the Emblem with the inscription: 'Royal Navy', 'The Handy Man', 'Royal Marine' and 'Soldiers of the Queen'.
Maker's mark: Williamsons, Longton, England. ($3\frac{1}{4}$ in. – 8.2 cm.)

(*All from the Oosthuizen Collection*)

General Ceramics 17

Plate 35
A pair of porcelain bulldogs.

Figure 1: With the wording 'Where's Krrruger?' on the base.

Figure 2: With the wording 'Who said Krrruger?' on the base.
Both unmarked. (6 in. – 15.2 cm.)
(*From the Oosthuizen Collection*)

Plate 36
An earthenware biscuit barrel with a picture of General Sir Redvers Buller in the uniform of the Colonel Commandant of the 60th Rifles.
Unmarked. ($6\frac{11}{16}$ in. – 177 cm.)
(*From the collection of Major Philip Erskine, Stellenbosch*)

Plate 37
Figure 1: A tobacco jar shaped in the form of the head of a British soldier.
Maker's mark: 8159. (6 in. – 15.2 cm.)

Boer War Memorabilia

Figure 2: A tobacco jar with pictures of 'Lord Kitchener', 'Sir Redvers Buller' and 'Lord Roberts' flanked by two soldiers.
The lid has a pewter clamp handle.
Maker's mark: Carlton Ware, Rd 352043, W & R, Stoke-on-Trent. (5½ in. – 14 cm.)

Figure 3: A tobacco jar shaped as the head of a City Imperial Volunteer with the letters 'C.I.V.' on the hat (lid).
Maker's mark: 8160 (6¼ in. – 15.9 cm.)
(*All from the collection of Mr Kenneth Griffith, London*)

Plate 38
Figure 1: A brown glaze milk jug with various war scenes and the following wording: 'South African War', 'They beat their swords into ploughshares' and 'Peace declared June 10 1902'.
Unmarked. (6 in. – 15.2 cm.)

Figure 2: A brown glaze teapot with pictures of the following generals: 'General Buller, Field Marshal Lord Roberts, Lord Kitchener, Col. Baden-Powell, Lt. Gen White' and

General Ceramics 19

below the pictures the words: 'Though it cost the best of our British blood there is no turning back.'
Unmarked. ($6\frac{1}{8}$ in. – 15.5 cm.)
(*From the Oosthuizen Collection*)

Plate 39
Figure 1: A pink lustre ware teapot with a picture of 'Lord Roberts'.
Unmarked. ($4\frac{1}{2}$ in. – 11.5 cm.)

Figure 2: Blue and mauve Wedgewood-style teapot with mouldings of Lord Roberts and Lord Kitchener on both sides.
Unmarked ($6\frac{1}{4}$ in. – 15.9 cm.)

Figure 3: A white lustre ware teapot with a picture in a medallion and the inscription 'General White'.
Unmarked. ($4\frac{1}{4}$ – 10.7 cm.)
(*All from the collection of Mr Kenneth Griffith, London*)

Plate 40
Figure 1: A President Kruger teapot.
Maker's mark: The Foley Intarsio England Rd. 363131. ($4\frac{3}{4}$ in. – 12.1 cm.)

20 Boer War Memorabilia

41

42

Figure 2: An Hon. Joseph Chamberlain teapot.
Maker's mark: The Foley Intarsio England Rd. 363131. (4¾ in. – 12.1 cm.)
(*Both from the collection of Mr Kenneth Griffith. London*)

Plate 41
The sketch from the publication *Ally Sloper's Half-holiday* was used on a great range of ceramics. The picture depicts General Roberts standing in front of a blackboard held by Lord Kitchener and wiping out the word 'Majuba'. Above the board the words 'Wiping something off-a-slate' and on the ribbon of the wreath 'Paardeberg'.

Figure 1: An ashtray with the picture.

Figure 2: A milk jug with the wording: 'Majuba February 27th 1881' and 'Paardeberg Feb. 27th 1900' with the above-mentioned picture on the reverse. (6 in. – 15.2 cm.)

Figure 3: A teapot with the picture on the front and the wording mentioned in Figure 2 on the reverse. (6¼ in. – 15.9 cm)
Maker's mark: W & R Stoke-on-Trent,

General Ceramics 21

43

Carlton Ware (Wiltshaw & Robinson Ltd.).
(*All from the Oosthuizen Collection*)

Plate 42
Rudyard Kipling's poem 'The Absent-minded Beggar' caught the public imagination. This poem was linked with the famous sketch 'A Gentleman in Kharki' by Caton Woodville and a large variety of ceramics with this combination was produced.

Figure 1: A teapot with the poem on the front and the sketch on the back.
$(5\frac{1}{2}$ in. -14 cm.)

Figure 2: A tray with the sketch and the poem.
$(11 \times 11$ in. -28×28 cm.)

Figure 3: A teapot with the sketch on front and the poem at the back.
All unmarked. $(5$ in. -12.7 cm.)
(*From the Oosthuizen Collection*)

Plate 43
Figure 1: A match holder with the 'A Gentleman in Kharki' sketch on front and the poem 'The Absent-minded Beggar' on the back.
Unmarked. $(2\frac{3}{4}$ in. -7 cm.)

Figure 2: A ceramic jug with the poem on the front and the sketch on the back.
Unmarked.

Figure 3: A small vase with the sketch on the front and the poem on the back.
Unmarked. $(4\frac{1}{2}$ in. $-11.4-$ cm$)$

Figure 4: A similar small jug.
Unmarked.

Figure 5: A similar cigarette holder.
Unmarked. $(2\frac{3}{4}$ in. -7 cm.)

Figure 6: A similar cup.
Unmarked. $(2\frac{3}{4}$ in. -7 cm.)

Figure 7: A similar milk jug.
Maker's mark: Macintyre 'J. M. & Co.' Burslem (James Macintyre & Co. Ltd.).
$(6\frac{1}{2}$ in. -16.5 cm.)

Figure 8: A similar small jug with a gold rim.
Unmarked.
(*All from the Oosthuizen Collection*)

Plate 44
A ceramic pipe tray with a round match holder.
In the centre a medal with a picture of Lord Roberts flanked by two soldiers with the wording: 'The Army' and 'Colonies — Supporters of the Empire — Volunteers'.
On the left a wreath with the names of 'Roberts, Buller, Kitchener, White, Baden-Powell. French'.
On the right a bugle with a banner with the words: 'An Empire Founded on Liberty'.

Figure 1: The tray. (10¼ in. – 26 cm.)

Figure 2: The match holder. (2¾ in. – 7 cm)
Maker's mark: the Foley Faience.
(*From the Oosthuizen Collection*)

Plate 45
A lustre ware cup and saucer. The cup with a picture of Queen Victoria and the saucer with pictures of 'Lieutenant-General J. D. P. French, General Right Hon. Sir Redvers H. Buller and Lieutenant-General Sir G. White'. A tea-set was produced with pictures of different generals on the ware.
(*From the collection of Major Philip Erskine, Stellenbosch*)

Plate 46
A Dutch cup and saucer with a picture of President Kruger and the wish '*Vergeet mij niet*' (forget me not).
(*By courtesy of the National Cultural History and Open-Air Museum, Pretoria*)

General Ceramics

Plate 47
A German pink lustre ware cup and saucer with a picture of 'President Kruger'.
Made in Bavaria.
(*By courtesy of the National Cultural History and Open-Air Museum, Pretoria*)

Plate 48
Figure 1: A pink lustre ware moustache cup with a picture of 'Col-Gen Baden-Powell'.
Unmarked.   ($3\frac{3}{8}$ in. – 8.6 cm.)

Centre collection: Three lustre ware egg cups with pictures of generals. 'Major-Gen. Lord Kitchener of Khartoum', 'Gen. Sir Redvers H. Buller' and 'Lieut-Gen Sir G. White'.
Unmarked.   ($2\frac{5}{8}$ in. – 6.7 cm)

Figure 3: A pink lustre ware tobacco jar (or biscuit jar) with pictures of the following: 'Lord Hector MacDonald, Lord Kitchener, Sir George White V.C., Lord Roberts V.C., Sir Redvers Buller V.C., Colonel Baden-Powell and General French'.
Unmarked   ($4\frac{3}{4}$ in. – 12.1 cm.)
(*From the Oosthuizen Collection*)

Plate 49

Figure 1: A sugar bowl with a picture of Lady Peace flanked by flags with the wording: 'Peace, Prosperity and Liberty for South Africa'.
Maker's mark: Crown Staffordshire.
(5½ in. – 14 cm. wide, 3 in. – 7.6 cm. high)

Figure 2: A European porcelain sugar bowl with a picture of President Kruger crossing the border to Mozambique with the wording: 'In memory of the late Transvaal Republic and Orange Free State' and 'Goodbye'.
Maker's mark: Britannia Porcelain Works, Karlsbad, Austria.   (4 in. – 10.2 cm.)
(*Both from the Oosthuizen Collection*)

Plate 50

The Allervale Pottery (near Torquay in Devon) issued many pieces of pottery in various shapes and different sizes with the following inscriptions: 'South Africa 1899–1900', 'God bless you Tommy Atkins' and 'Here's your country's love to you'.

Figure 1: A milk jug.   (4 in. – 8.6 cm.)

Figure 2: A small loving cup.
(3⅜ in. – 8.6 cm.)

Figure 3: A mug.   (4¼ in. – 10.8 cm.)
Maker's mark: (Impressed) Aller Vale Pottery.   (*From the Oosthuizen Collection*)

General Ceramics 25

Plate 51
A blue ground stoneware vase decorated in white with applied moulded portraits of Lord Kitchener and Lord Roberts between crossed rifles.
 A similar vase was also made with picures of Sir Redvers Buller and Colonel Baden-Powell.
Maker's impressed mark: Dudson England.
($7\frac{1}{8}$ in. – 18 cm.)
(*From the collection of Major Philip Erskine, Stellenbosch*)

Plate 52
Four unmarked European porcelain pieces — three small vases and a perfume bottle. Two items with a picture of President Kruger and the wording: 'Paul Kruger' and '*President der Zuid-Afrikaansche Republiek*' (President of the South African Republic). Two items with a picture of General Joubert and the wording: 'Piet Joubert' and '*Opperbevelhebber der Transvaalsche Troepen*' (Commander-in-Chief of the Transvaal Forces).
(*By courtesy of the National Cultural History and Open-Air Museum, Pretoria*)

Plate 53
Two unmarked European porcelain perfume bottles with pewter stoppers and pictures of Boer leaders.

Figure 1: With a picture of General Joubert and the wording 'Piet Joubert' and '*Opperbevelhebber der Transvaalsche Troepen*' (Commander-in-Chief of the Transvaal Forces).

Figure 2: With a picture of President Kruger and the wording: 'Paul Kruger' and '*President der Zuid-Afrikaansche Republiek*' (President of the South African Republic).
($3\frac{1}{4}$ in. – 8.3 cm.)
(*From the Oosthuizen Collection*)

26 Boer War Memorabilia

53

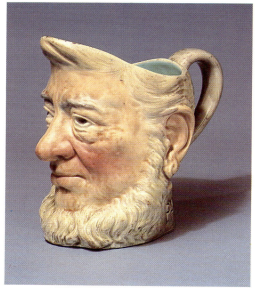

54

Plate 54
A European pottery character jug of President Kruger.
Maker's mark: Sarreguemines.
(7 in. – 17.8 cm.)
Smaller similar jugs were also produced.
(*From the Oosthuizen Collection*)

Plate 55
Figure 1: A character jug of President Kruger with a crown at the back of his top hat. On the band of the hat the words 'H. M. Oom Paul'.
Unmarked. ($5\frac{7}{8}$ in. – 15 cm.)

Figure 2: A plate with a light green and gold border and in black the emblem of the South African Republic (ZAR).
Unmarked. ($5\frac{1}{2}$ in. – 14 cm)

General Ceramics

Figure 3: A character jug of President Kruger with a pipe as handle.
Unmarked. (7⅞ in – 20 cm.)
(*All from the Oosthuizen Collection*)

Plate 56
A set of six plates made in France. The plates were also produced with different coloured borders. All the plates have the words '*Au Transvaal*' at the top of the picture in the centre.

Figure 1: Plate 3 '*Un Boër de France — Le Colonel de Villebois-Mareuil*'.

Figure 2: Plate 2 '*Anglais executant un mouvement tournant*'.

Figure 3: Plate 1 '*Le Colosse de Cecil Rhodes*'. The other plates in the series are inscribed as follows.

Plate 4: '*Pugnant en blanc un Zoulou pour en faire un Highlander*'.

Plate 5: '*Avez vous feutale de vos canons*'.

Plate 6: '*Pleurez pas Kitty! Je vous promets de me faire faire prisonnier*'.

Maker's mark: Terre de Fer H.B & Cie.
(7⅝ in. – 19.3 cm.)
(*From the colleection of Mr Kenneth Griffith, London*)

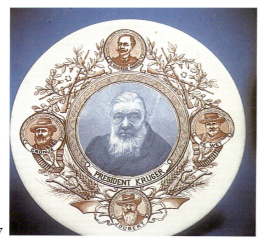

Plate 57

A European earthenware plate. In the centre a picture of President Kruger and around the border pictures of Boer generals: 'De Villebois-Mareuil, De Wet, Joubert and Cronje'.
Maker's mark: Sarreguemines.
(8½ in. – 21.6 cm.)
(*By courtesy of Rita and Ian Smythe, Britannia, London*)

Plate 58

Figure 1: A Belgian ceramic milk jug with a full-length picture of the Boer General de Wet.

Maker's mark: Villeroy & Bosch, Wallerfangen. (8 in. – 20.3 cm.)

Figure 2: Cup with a picture of Commandant Beyers.
(*By courtesy of the War Museum of the Boer Republics, Bloemfontein*)

Plate 59

A sauce boat with the emblem of the Orange Free State Republic.
(*By courtesy of the War Museum of the Boer Republics, Bloemfontein*)

Plate 60

A Portuguese ceramic plate with a decorated border and the following words in the centre: 'J. J. Claase Alcobaca 16.5.1901 Portugal;
(6 in. – 15.2 cm.)
(*By courtesy of the War Museum of the Boer Republics, Bloemfontein*)

Plate 61
A large Portuguese ceramic plate with flowers around the border and a picture of General Joubert in the centre and with the title: 'General Joubert 1900'. (13 in. – 33 cm.)
(*By courtesy of the National Cultural History and Open-Air Museum, Pretoria*)

medal and around the border the words: '*Anglo-Boere Oorlog* 1899 1902 *Alles sal reg kom*' (all will turn out well).
Maker's mark: Schoonhoven, Holland.
(7⅞ in. – 20 cm.)
(*By courtesy of the National Cultural History and Open-Air Museum, Pretoria*)

Plate 62
A French ceramic plate decorated with the flags of the Boer Republics and the words: '*Aux honneur Boers*'. (9½ in. – 24.1 cm.)
(*By courtesy of the National Cultural History and Open-Air Museum, Pretoria*)

Plate 63
A Dutch ceramic plate. In the centre pictures of the '*Anglo-Boere Oorlog*' commemorative

Plate 64
A German porcelain plate with a picture of a man being attacked by a swarm of bees with the slogan: '*Eendracht maakt Macht*' (unity is strength).
Maker's mark: Bomm Porzelan Werken.
(approx. 7½ in. – 19 cm.)
(*By courtesy of the National Cultural History and Open-Air Museum, Pretoria*)

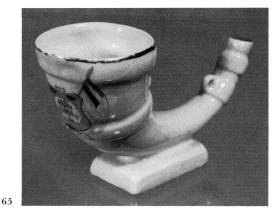

Plate 65
An unmarked ceramic powder horn with the Orange Free State coat-of-arms.
(*By courtesy of the National Cultural History and Open-Air Museum, Pretoria*)

Plate 66
Dutch ceramics with blue flowers and pictures of Boer generals.

Figure 1: A tumbler with a picture of 'L. Botha'.

Figure 2: A jug with a picture of 'C. H. de Wet'.

Figure 3: A tumbler with a picture of 'J. H. de la Rey'.
(*By courtesy of the National Cultural History and Open-Air Museum, Pretoria*)

Plate 67
A Dutch ceramic tray with blue flowers and pictures of the Boer Presidents 'M. T. Steyn' and 'S. J. P. Kruger'.

General Ceramics 31

Maker's mark: Societe Ceramique Maastricht, Holland.
(*By courtesy of the National Cultural History and Open-Air Museum, Pretoria*)

Plate 68
A Dutch ceramic jug with a picture of President and Mrs Kruger in front of their home and the words: '*Met beste geluk wenschen Van Schoch & Co., Rustenburg*' (with best wishes Van Schoch & Co., Rustenburg).
($6\frac{1}{2}$ in. – 16.5 cm.)
(*By courtesy of the National Cultural History and Open-Air Museum, Pretoria*)

Plate 69
A set of Dutch plates depicting scenes from the Boer War. The plates are all marked on the back with the word '*Boeren*'.
Maker's mark: Petrus Regout & Co. Maastricht. ($7\frac{5}{8}$ in. – 19.4 cm.)
(*From the Oosthuizen Collection*)

Plate 70
A German earthenware tobacco jar with the figure of General de Wet holding Lord Kitchener over a globe. On the globe the markings: Transvaal, Orange Freistaat and Natal.
Unmarked. ($7\frac{3}{8}$ in. – 18.7 cm.)
(*From the Oosthuizen Collection*)

Plate 71

Figure 1: A small jug with two handles with the coat-of-arms of the Transvaal.
Maker's mark: Gemma.
(1 3/8 in. – 3.5 cm.)

Figure 2: A 'Goss' model of a Boer War Memorial.
On the front: a coat-of-arms with markings 'Craignez Honte', Duke of Portland, Ashington & Hirst.
On the back: 'Erected in Honour of Regulars Reserves and Volunteers of Ashington Urban District who served their country in South Africa 1902'.
Maker's mark: Willow Art China Longton Staffordshire.   (5 1/2 in. – 14 cm.)

(*Figure 1 from the collection of Mr Kenneth Griffith, London; Figure 2 from the Oosthuizen Collection*)

General Ceramics 33

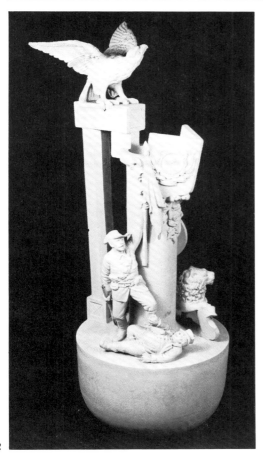

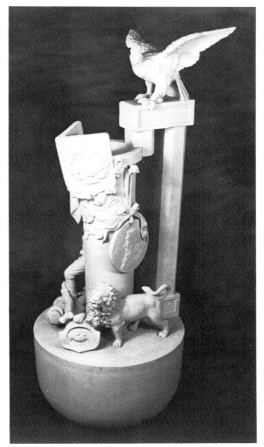

Plate 72 and 73
A rare Portuguese jug, one of a number manufactured at the request of Avelino A. S. Bello in honour of the two Boer Republics. These were made in 1901, when there were Boers in internment camps in Portugal.
On the lip of the jug are the coats-of-arms of the two Boer Republics. On one of its sides is the figure of a Boer with his foot on John Bull. On the other side, under a medallion of President Kruger, is a lion with one foot on a shield with the motto '*Eewige Broederband*' (Everlasting Bond of Brothers). Under the eagle is the motto '*Leve Kruger en Steyn moge de Zuid Afrikaanshe Strydmachten overwinnen*' (long live Kruger and Steyn, may the South African Forces conquer).
(*By courtesy of the War Museum of the Boer Republics, Bloemfontein.*)

CHAPTER 2

Character Figures, Busts and Statuettes

Porcelain figures, Staffordshire figures, bisque figures, Goss and Parian ware figures

In the ceramic field a number of porcelain Boer War-related figures were produced by the leading manufacturers. The Staffordshire Potteries also produced a great number of mounted figures of Boer War generals.

Parian ware Boer War figures were produced. Parian ware was introduced in 1846 by the Copeland Manufactory for the reproduction of marble statues on a small scale and at a low cost. The marble-like paste resembles the Parian Marbles, and is a versatile body capable of being moulded into intricate shapes. It was used for many types of articles, normally white and unglazed.

A range called Goss ware was also produced. The English potter William Henry Goss started the Falcon Factory in Stoke-on-Trent in 1858, and manufactured parian ware amongst other products. In 1934 the company was renamed Goss China Co. Ltd. The factory is well known for the manufacture of popular souvenir china.

The ceramic manufacturers also made 'bisque figures'. Biscuit or unglazed porcelain figures were first made around 1751 at Vincennes and Sèvres in France. The principal manufactory for biscuit figures in England was in Derby. In contrast to hard-paste porcelain figures, biscuit figures of soft paste, or pâte tendre, are smooth to the touch and have a warm soft tone.

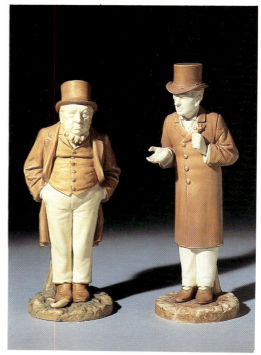

Plate 74
A brown and green glaze figure of a British soldier.
Maker: Doulton Lambeth, England.
$(12\frac{1}{4}$ in. – 31.1 cm.)
(*From the Oosthuizen Collection*)

Plate 75
Figure 1: A Worcester porcelain figure of President Paul Kruger. $(8\frac{1}{8}$ in. – 21 cm.)

Figure 2: A Worcester porcelain figure of Colonial Secretary Joseph Chamberlain.
$(8\frac{3}{4}$ in. – 22.2 cm.)
Maker's mark: Hadley's Worcester.
(*Both from the Oosthuizen Collection*)

Plate 76
Worcester porcelain figures of British soldiers. They range in height from $7\frac{1}{2}$ in. to $7\frac{3}{4}$ in. (19 cm. to 19.7 cm.).

Figure 1: 'Colonial Trooper' Royal Worcester No. 2108.

Figure 2: 'Black Watch' Royal Worcester No. 2109.

Figure 3: 'Imperial Yeoman' Royal Worcester No. 2107.
Other figures made by the Royal Worcester factory:
'Imperial Forces' No. 2106;
'Handy Man' No. 2110;
'Guardsman' No. 2111.
(*All from the Oosthuizen Collection*)

Plate 77
Figure 1: An unmarked ceramic bust of the 'Earl Kitchener'. $(5\frac{1}{2}$ in. – 14 cm.)

Figure 2: A white ceramic bust of Lord Kitchener.
Marked: A. (8 in. – 20.3 cm.)

Figure 3: An unmarked ceramic character jug of Lord Kitchener. (7 in. – 17.8 cm.)
(*All from the Oosthuizen Collection*)

Character Figures, Busts and Statuettes

76

77

Plate 78
Figure 1: A ceramic comic figure of President Kruger.
Maker's mark: R. P., C. H. Brannam, Barnstaple 1400. (5¾ in. – 14.6 cm.)

Figure 2: A President Kruger porcelain money box (identical to the metal money box in Plate 103). Unmarked. (5½ in. – 14 cm.)

Figure 3: A green glaze character jug of President Kruger with a 'boar' on the back with the tusks of the boar as handle.
Impressed: 426. (6 in. – 15.2 cm.)
(*All from the collection of Mr Kenneth Griffith, London*)

Plate 79
A colourful porcelain figure of Major General Baden-Powell, the Founder of the Scout Movement, with his dog.
Maker's mark: Copeland Spode, England. (10 in. – 25.4 cm.)
(*By courtesy of The Scout Association, Baden-Powell House, London*)

Plate 80
A ceramic character flask of President Kruger. On the base: 'Ohm Paul'. The top-hat is the lid.
(*By courtesy of the National Cultural History and Open-Air Museum, Pretoria*)

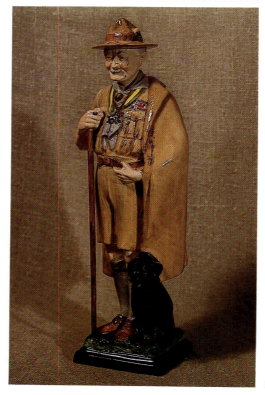

Plate 81
A ceramic tobacco jar of President Kruger sitting on a tree stump.
(*By courtesy of the National Cultural History and Open-Air Museum, Pretoria*)

Character Figures, Busts and Statuettes

80
81

82

Plate 82
Figure 1: A Staffordshire figure of 'Lord Dundonald' on a horse. (14½ in. – 36.9 cm.)

Figure 2: Staffordshire figure of 'Baden-Powell' on a horse. (12½ in. – 31.8 cm.)

Figure 3: Staffordshire figure of 'Hector Macdonald' on a horse. (12½ in. – 31.8 cm.)
(*All from the Oosthuizen Collection*)

40 Boer War Memorabilia

83

84

Plate 83

Figure 1: Staffordshire figure of 'Kitchener' on a horse. (14¾ in. – 37.5 cm.)

Figure 2: Staffordshire figure of 'Buller' on a horse. (14½ in. – 36.9 cm.)
(*Both from the Oosthuizen Collection*)

Plate 84

Figure 1: Staffordshire figure of 'French' on a horse facing right. (14½ in. – 36.9 cm.)

Figure 2: Staffordshire figure of 'Roberts' on a horse facing left. (14½ in. – 36.9 cm.)
(*Both from the Oosthuizen Collection*)

Character Figures, Busts and Statuettes 41

Plate 85
Figure 1: Staffordshire figure of 'Lord Roberts' on a horse. (11¼ in. – 28.5 cm.)

Figure 2: Staffordshire figure of 'Roberts' on a horse. (14½ in. – 36.9 cm.)

Figure 3: Staffordshire figure of 'Lord Roberts' on a horse. (12 in. – 30.5 cm.)
(*All from the Oosthuizen Collection*)

Plate 86
Figure 1: Staffordshire figure of 'Sir Redvers Buller' on a horse. (12 in. – 30.5 cm.)

Figure 2: Staffordshire figure of General Buller' on a horse. (10½ in. – 26.7 cm.)

Figure 3: Staffordshire figure of 'Major Macdonald' on a horse. (11 in. – 28 cm.)
(*All from the Oosthuizen Collection*)

Plate 87

Figure 1: A standing Staffordshire figure of 'Roberts'. (14 in. – 35.5 cm.)

Figure 2: A standing Staffordshire figure of 'Kitchener'. (14 in. – 35.5 cm.)

Figure 3: A colourful standing figure of 'Kitchener'. (14½ in. – 36.8 cm.)
(*All from the Oosthuizen Collection*)

Plate 88

The Staffordshire potters produced the same figure to honour two different generals; the first figure, to honour the Hero of Mafeking, is marked 'Baden-Powell', the second to honour the Boer General, is marked 'De Wet'.
(Both figures 17 in. – 43.2 cm.)
(*From the Oosthuizen Collection*)

Character Figures, Busts and Statuettes

Plate 89
'The Peace' Staffordshire figure. A Boer and John Bull are shaking hands in front of an Angel. The Angel holds a ribbon inscribed 'Peace on earth goodwill towards men'. Below the three figures the words 'Boer War — Peace Declared — June 1st 1902'.
(12½ in. – 31.7 cm.)
(*By courtesy of the Antique Collector's Club*)

Plate 90
A large Parian ware bust. The inscription on the base reads:
'Lord Roberts V.C. G.C.B.'.
(21 in. – 53.3 cm.)
(*From the collection of Mr Kenneth Griffith, London*)

Plate 91
A standing Parian ware figure of Lord Roberts. Inscribed on the base:
'Lord Roberts V.C. C.G.B.' and marked on the back:
'W. C. Lawton Sculptor, August 31st 1900, Copyright'. (11 in. – 28 cm.)
(*By courtesy of Rita & Ian Smythe, Britannia, London*)

44 Boer War Memorabilia

92

93

Character Figures, Busts and Statuettes

94

Plate 92

Figure 1: A Parian bust of 'General White' as inscribed on the base. On the back: 'By W. C. Lawton Scul (ptor), Copyright, Feb 24th 1900'. (8¼ in. – 21 cm.)

Figure 2: A Parian bust of 'General Buller' as inscribed on the base. On the back: 'By W. C. Lawton Scul (ptor), Copyright, Oct 30, 1899'. (8¼ in. – 21 cm.)

Figure 3: A Parian bust of 'Lord Roberts' as inscribed on the base. On the back: 'By W. C. Lawton Scul (ptor), Copyright, Jan 1900'. (8¼ in. – 21 cm.)

(*All from the Oosthuizen Collection*)

Plate 93

Figure 1: A small bust of Lord Kitchener inscribed 'Kitchener'.
Maker's mark: 1209. (5⅛ in. – 13 cm.)

Figure 2: A small Parian ware bust of Lord Kitchener with a white glazed base. The inscription on the back: 'Lord Kitchener' and 'W. G. Lawton Scul (ptor), Copyright'. (6⅜ in. – 16.2 cm.)

(*Both from the Oosthuizen Collection*)

Plate 94

A selection of bisque figures.

Figure 1: A small figure of 'A Gentleman in Kharki' with his hat on. (4¾ in. – 12.1 cm.)

Figure 2: 'A Gentleman in Kharki' on the base of the soldier figure. (5¾ in. – 14.7 cm.)

Figure 3: A seated wounded soldier. (6 in. – 15.2 cm.)

Figure 4: Standing soldier, on the base the inscription 'Duty'. (5¾ in. – 14.7 cm.)

Figure 5: A Royal Marine. On the base the inscription 'The Handyman'. (6 in. – 15.2 cm.)

Figure 6: A standing figure of Lord Roberts, the base inscribed 'Old Bobs'. (5¾ in. – 14.7 cm.)

Figure 7: A standing figure of a City Imperial Volunteer. (7½ in. – 19 cm.)

(*All from the collection of Mr Kenneth Griffith, London*)

46 Boer War Memorabilia

Plate 95

Figure 1: A bisque figure of a soldier.
(8½ in. – 21.6 cm.)

Figure 2: A colourful bisque figure of 'Lord Roberts'. (8½ in. – 21.6 cm.)

Figure 3: A bisque figure of a Handyman.
(8 in. – 20.3 cm.)

Figure 4: A bisque figure of a nurse.
(9 in. – 22.8 cm.)

Figure 5: A bisque figure of a soldier.
(5¾ in. – 14.6 cm.)

Figure 6: A bisque model of a soldier.
(8¼ in. – 21 cm.)
(*All from the Oosthuizen Collection*)

Plate 96
A standing bisque figure of a soldier.
(*By courtesy of the National Army Museum, London*)

Character Figures, Busts and Statuettes 47

Plate 97
A pair of spelter lamps made in France. A British soldier with a gun and a Boer soldier with a gun and map.
Made by Rousseau.

(26½ in. – 67.3 cm.)
(From the collection of Mr Kenneth Griffith, London)

Boer War Memorabilia

Plate 98
A figure of a marine with a cannon.
Maker's mark: Pattern 1430, Biscuit Porcelain. ($4\frac{1}{2}$ in. – 11.4 cm.)
(*By courtesy of Rita & Ian Smythe, Britannia, London*)

Plate 99
Character statuettes of generals with the maker's inscription:
'Sidney March SC and Copyright Elkington & Co. Ltd.'.

Figure 1: Baden-Powell. The inscription on the base: 'Mafeking 1900'.
($8\frac{3}{8}$ in. – 21.3 cm.)

Figure 2: Buller. The inscription on the base 'Natal 1900'. (9 in. – 22.9 cm.)

Figure 3: Roberts. The inscription on the base 'Pretoria 1900'. ($8\frac{1}{16}$ in. – 20.5 cm.)

Figure 4: Kekewich. The inscription on the base: 'Kimberley 1900'. ($8\frac{1}{2}$ in. – 21 cm.)
These figures were all recast later without markings on the bases.
(*By permission of the National Army Museum, London*)

Character Figures, Busts and Statuettes

Plate 100
A bronze character figure of Cecil John Rhodes, signed by Vernon March and dated 1901. ($9\frac{5}{8}$ in. – 24.5 cm.)
(*By courtesy of Sotheby's, Johannesburg*)

Plate 101
A bronze character statuette of a City Imperial Volunteer on a horse.
The inscription on the base 'C.I.V.'.
(12 in. – 30.5 cm.)
(*By courtesy of the Africana Museum, Johannesburg*)

Plate 102

Figure 1: A bronze 'A Gentleman in Kharki' figure. ($9\frac{3}{4}$ in. – 23.5 cm.)

Figure 2: A bronze inkwell — a soldier behind a rock. (3 in. – 7.6 cm.)

Figure 3 & 5: A pair of bronze candlesticks with standing British soldiers.
(9 in. – 22.9 cm.)

50 Boer War Memorabilia

102

Figure 4: A bronze figure of a City Imperial Volunteer. ($9\frac{1}{4}$ in. – 23.5 cm.)

Figure 6: A bronze figure of a marine with the inscription: 'The Handyman'.
(11 in. – 28 cm.)
(*From the collection of Mr Kenneth Griffith, London*)

Plate 103

Figure 1: A caricature money box depicting President Kruger.
On the hat the inscription: 'Transvaal money box' and on the back:
'By permission of the proprietors of the Westminster Gazette' and 'Made in England'. ($6\frac{1}{2}$ in. – 16.5 cm.)

Figure 2: A brass imitation of the box in Figure 1 currently being reproduced and sold in the USA. ($5\frac{1}{2}$ in. – 14 cm.)
(*From the Oosthuizen Collection*)

Plate 104

Figure 1: A spelter bust of Lord Kitchener on a wood base inscribed:
'Kitchener'.
Unmarked. ($7\frac{1}{4}$ in. – 18.4 cm.)

Figure 2: A bronze bust of Lord Roberts on a marble base.
Unmarked. ($8\frac{1}{4}$ in. – 21 cm.)

Figure 3: A spelter bust with the inscription 'Lord Roberts' on a wood base.
Unmarked. ($7\frac{1}{4}$ in. – 18.4 cm.)
(*All from the Oosthuizen Collection*)

Character Figures, Busts and Statuettes 51

103

104

CHAPTER 3

Model Soldiers

Miniature models

Human-scale model soldiers were buried in the ancient graves in China. Miniature model soldiers were also found in the ancient tombs in Egypt. Flat lead model soldiers were manufactured for many centuries in Germany and France. In 1893 an English manufacturer, William Britain, started the manufacture of hollow figures made from an alloy lighter and cheaper than lead. By the turn of the century many models were being produced by Britain at his factory.

Of interest to Boer War memorabilia collectors are several important sets manufactured by Britain's. To represent the Boer side the company made two sets — Boer Cavalry and Boer Infantry.

Britain's set No. 6: Boer Cavalry
The cavalry set had five figures in the box: four figures with fixed arms carrying rifles and their leader aiming a revolver. All the figures wear black hats. This issue is very rare.

Britain's set No. 26: Boer Infantry
The infantry set first appeared as swiftly cobbled figures based on the basic British infantryman, with rifles at the slope. In 1906 they were changed to become more warlike figures, standing with bayoneted rifles at the ready, while their officer held sword and pistol. These figures also had black hats. This set is also very rare.

Britain's manufactured several different sets to cover the British side.

Britain's set No. 38: Dr Jameson and the South African Mounted Infantry
The set was issued around the Boer War period. Dr Jameson holds a revolver. His name did not appear on the box lid for long, and later issues had an anonymous officer. These figures are very rare.

Britain's set no. 77: Gordon Highlanders
The Gordons are marching figures, at slope, with white hats and colourful tartans.

Britain's set No. 79: Naval Landing Party
The Naval landing party set contains a petty officer and eight bluejackets pulling a quick-firer and limber.

Britain's set No. 96: York and Lancaster Regiment
The York and Lancaster Regiment has soldiers in red tunics, running at trail.

Britain's set No. 104: City Imperial Volunteers (CIV)
The City Imperial Volunteer set contains nine soldiers plus an officer, all in khaki with slouch hats. They were first issued in 1900 and revived in 1930.

Britian's set No. 105: Imperial Yeomanry
The Imperial Yeomanry set contains cavalry figures, in khaki with slouch hats and bandoliers. There are five figures in a set. They were also reissued in 1930.

Britian's set No. 109: Dublin Fusiliers
In this set the Dublin Fusiliers are marching at trail in khaki uniform.

Britain's set No. 110: Devonshire Regiment
The Devonshire Regiment is also in khaki and marching at slope.

Britain's set No. 118: Gordon Highlanders
In this set the Gordons are lying firing. They wear red tunics and tartans. These figures were manufactured in vast quantities.

Britain's set No. 119: Gloucestershire Regiment
The Gloucestershire figures are standing firing in khaki uniform.

The City Imperial Volunteer figures were the first to carry a date and copyright identification in the form of a paper sticker. The prices for the boxes of cavalry and infantry were 'one shilling' or 'one shilling and twopence'.

Until the beginning of the First World War Britain's systematically reissued many of the models with improvements in quality of anatomy. Britain's also produced a very rare Boer War waggon supply column. In 1905 a 4.7 in. naval gun firing shells or matchsticks was produced — it harked back to the naval guns landed in Natal by the men of the cruisers HMS *Terrible, Powerful, Monarch* and *Doris*.

European countries also produced Boer War models. In 1902 the German firm Ammon of Nuremberg produced a British armoured train. The set contains a locomotive and several three-dimensional waggons manned by 45 mm. semi-round British troops in khaki. The firm of Heyde in Dresden marketed its field railway (in British uniforms) after the use of armoured trains in the Boer War.

In recent years a number of manufacturers have started to issue Boer War figures. A number of private model-makers are also turning out a small number of figures of high quality.

Plate 105
A very rare Britain's set of an army supply column, produced at the time of the Boer War and modelled on the uniforms of the City Imperial Volunteers.
(*Photograph by courtesy of Phillips, the international fine art auctioneers, London*)

Plate 106
A naval landing party consisting of eight bluejackets, led by a petty officer, pulling a quickfirer and limber.
(*Photograph by courtesy of Mr Peter Johnson. Curator of the Forbes Magazine Museum of Military Miniatures, Tangier, Morocco*)

Model Soldiers 55

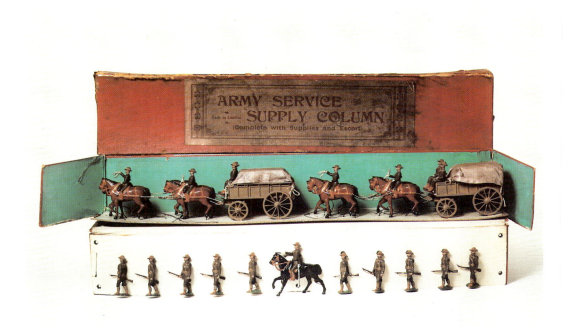

105

106

Boer War Memorabilia

107

108

Plate 107
A representation by Henry Harris, model-maker, of a Boer War, bullock-drawn naval landing party. Made in the 1950s or 1960s, and mainly conversions from Britain's models, including the famous Britain's 4.7 in. naval gun.
(Photograph by courtesy of Mr Peter Johnson, Curator of the Forbes Magazine Museum of Military Miniatures, Tangier, Morocco)

Plate 108
Modern models of soldiers currently being made by Ken Kearsley of England in London.

Figure 1: A '1900 British Infantry' soldier.
(4 in. – 10.1 cm.)

Figure 2: A small figure of a 'Lancashire Fusilier'.
($2\frac{3}{8}$ in. – 6 cm.)

Model Soldiers 57

Figure 3: A '1900 Black Watch Regt.' soldier. (4 in. – 10.1 cm.)

Figure 4: A small figure marked 'Imperial Yeomanry'. ($2\frac{3}{8}$ in. – 6 cm.)

Figure 5: A model of a 'C.I.V.' (on hat) soldier with the marking '1900 Imperial Yeomanry'. (4 in. – 10.1 cm.)

Figure 6: A small model of a 'Boer soldier' with a gun on his back. ($2\frac{3}{8}$ in. – 6 cm.)

Figure 7: A model soldier marked '1900 2nd Irish Rifles'. (4 in. – 10.1 cm.)

All the figures carry the maker's mark: Ken Kearsley, England.
(*All from the Oosthuizen Collection*)

Plate 109
This display of the Royal Engineers' Observation Section was assembled by a collector using large amounts of recasts. It is on display in the Forbes Museum of Military Miniatures in Tangier, Morocco.
(*Photograph by courtesy of Mr Peter Johnson, Curator of the Forbes Magazine Museum of Military Miniatures, Tangier, Morrocco*)

58 Boer War Memorabilia

Plate 110
The Boer Infantry set from Britain's. The set is very rare.
(*Photograph by courtesy of Phillips, the international fine art auctioneers, London*)

CHAPTER 4

Glassware

Plates, glasses, paperweights, rolling-pins and busts

During the Victorian era the glass industry saw a great expansion as mechanization increased. The development of press-moulded glass, which was cheaper to manufacture, was responsible for the general introduction of glassware into the homes of the majority of the people.

By the end of the Victorian era — the period during which the Boer War took place — the variety of glass products available ranged from expensive cut and engraved table glass to mass-produced pressed-glass.

Very few manufacturers marked their products with their names.

Many of the Boer War memorabilia glass items carry acid-etched decorations. Acid-etching was a popular method used by the end of the nineteenth century.

Many different kinds of glass items were produced, and this variety is reflected in the range of Boer War memorabilia.

Plate 111
A wine goblet etched with a picture of President Kruger. This was used by President Kruger at a banquet in Paris in his honour.
(*By permission of the Africana Museum, Johannesburg*)

112

113

Plate 112

Figure 1: A pressed-glass plate. Around the border the wording 'Baden-Powell — Mafeking'. In the centre, between two crossed flags, the inscription 'Besieged 7 months — V.R. — 17 May 1900 Relieved'.

(10¼ in. – 26 cm.)

Figure 2: A pressed-glass plate. Around the border the wording 'Roberts — V.R. — Pretoria' and in the centre, between two crossed flags, 'Entered June 5 1900'.

(10¼ in. – 26 cm.)

(Both from the Oosthuizen Collection)

Plate 113

Three tumblers with etched pictures.

Figure 1: With an etched picture of 'President Steyn' with the Orange Free State coat-of-arms below the picture.

Figure 2: With an etched picture of President Kruger above the Transvaal coat-of-arms.

Figure 3: With an etched picture of 'Generaal de la Rey'.

(By courtesy of the National Cultural History and Open-Air Museum, Pretoria)

Glassware 61

Plate 114
Figure 1: A tumbler with a picture of 'A Gentleman in Kharki' transfer-printed on the glass.
($4\frac{3}{8}$ in. – 11.1 cm.)

Figure 2: A tumbler with medallion picture transfer printed on the glass and the inscription 'Field-Marshal Lord Roberts V.C.'.
($4\frac{1}{2}$ in. – 11.4 cm.)

Figure 3: A champagne flute engraved with a medallion picture between two crossed flags with the inscription 'B.P.' and 'Hero of Mafeking'.
(8 in. – 20.3 cm.)

Figure 4: A tumbler, transfer-printed with a medallion picture and the inscription 'General Lord Kitchener'.
($4\frac{1}{4}$ in. – 10.8 cm.)

Figure 5: Printed on this glass the words: 'Cronje Surrendered Feb.y 27th 1900 — Lord Roberts — Lord Kitchener — For English Fruit Preserving Co's J.P.'.
($4\frac{3}{4}$ in. – 12.1 cm.)
(*From the Oosthuizen Collection*)

Plate 115
A glass rolling-pin, with a gilt background and printed portraits of 'British Leaders in the Transvaal War 1899–1900'. The pictures are of General Baden-Powell, Lord Roberts and General Buller.
(Diameter $5\frac{1}{4}$ in. – 13 cm., Length $15\frac{1}{4}$ in. – 40 cm.)
(*By permission of the Africana Museum, Johannesburg; photograph by courtesy of Sotheby's, Johannesburg*)

Plate 116

Figure 1: A round glass paperweight with a picture of General Baden-Powell affixed to the back. ($2\frac{3}{8}$ in. – 6 cm.)
(*From the collection of Mr Kenneth Griffith, London*)

Figure 2: A square paperweight with a picture of General Buller affixed to the back. ($4 \times 2\frac{1}{2}$ in. – 10.2 × 6.5 cm.)
(*By courtesy of Rita & Ian Smythe, Britannia, London*)

Figure 3: A round glass paperweight with a picture of Queen Victoria surrounded by pictures of six Boer War generals affixed to the back. (2 in. – 5 cm.)
(*From the Oosthuizen Collection*)

Plate 117

A German opaque glass bust of President Kruger with incorrect moulded words: '*Präs. d. Kap Kolonie*' (President of the Cape Colony). (5 in. – 12.7 cm.)
(*By courtesy of the National Cultural History and Open-Air Museum, Pretoria*)

Plate 118
Two of a series of glasses distributed by the English Fruit Preserving Co.

Figure 1: A glass with a printed picture of General Baden-Powell and his name 'Baden-Powell'. ($4\frac{3}{4}$ in. – 12.1 cm.)

Figure 2: A glass with a printed picture under the name 'Lord Kitchener' and the name of the company. ($4\frac{3}{4}$ in. – 12.1 cm.)
(*In the collection of Major Philip Erskine, Stellenbosch*)

Plate 119
Tumblers used by the 'Cafe Transvalia' in Rotterdam at the turn of the century. The glasses have pictures of Presidents Steyn and Kruger.
(*By courtesy of the War Museum of the Boer Republics, Bloemfontein*)

Plate 120
A French opaque glass bust of President Kruger. Moulded on the base the words '*Guerre aux Tyrans*' and 'Kruger'.
($11\frac{13}{16}$ in. – 30 cm.)
(*By courtesy of Sotheby's, Johannesburg*)

CHAPTER 5

Stamps and Covers

Postage stamps, war covers, POW covers, postmarks and censors' marks

During the Boer War many of the soldiers engaged in South Africa bought and collected used and unused postage stamps and envelopes and covers to take home with them as souvenirs or for their stamp collections.

STAMPS
Today many collectors of Boer War memorabilia are collecting stamps from the various territories in South Africa, issued during the 1899–1902 period.

Cape of Good Hope Stamps (Cape Colony)
The following stamps were in use in the Cape during the Boer war.
(*a*) Issue of 1884–1898 marked 'Cape of Good Hope' (with Hope seated):
  $\frac{1}{2}$d. grey-black
  $\frac{1}{2}$d. green
  1d. rose
  2d. bistre
  2d. chocolate-brown
  3d. red-violet
  4d. blue
  4d. pale olive-green
  6d. violet
  1s. green
  1s. blue-green
  1s. yellow-buff
  5s. orange
  5s. brown-orange

In 1891 the 3d. violet rose stamp was surcharged with '2$\frac{1}{2}$d.'.
In 1892–1896 the following stamps were added to this issue:
  2$\frac{1}{2}$d. olive-green
  2$\frac{1}{2}$d. ultramarine
  2$\frac{1}{2}$d. bistre overstamped 'one penny'

(*b*) Isssue of 1893–1902 marked 'Cape of Good Hope' (with Hope standing):
  $\frac{1}{2}$d. green
  1d. rose
  3d. violet

(*c*) Issue of 1900 marked 'Cape of Good Hope' (with Table Mountain and Bay and coat-of-arms):
  1d. carmine-rose

(d) Issue of 1902 marked 'Cape of Good Hope' (with King Edward VII):
    ½d. emerald
    1d. carmine-rose
    2d. brown
    1s. bistre

Mafeking
The following stamps were issued in Mafeking during the Siege of Mafeking, October 1899 to May 1900.

(a) Cape of Good Hope stamps surcharged and marked 'Mafeking besieged':
    1d. surcharge on ½d. green
    3d. surcharge on 1d. rose
    6d. surcharge on 3d. red-violet
    1s. surcharge on 4d. pale olive-green

(b) Bechuanaland Protectorate stamps surcharged and marked 'Mafeking besieged':
    1d. surcharge on 1d. lilac
    6d. surcharge on 2d. green and carmine
    6d. surcharge on 3d. violet and yellow
    6d. surcharge on 3d. violet
    1s. surcharge on 4d. brown and green
    1s. surcharge on 6d. violet – rose
    2s. surcharge on 1s. green

(c) Issue of 1900 (photographic print):
    1d. blue marked 'Siege of Mafeking' (man on bicycle: Sergeant-Major Goodyear)
    3d. blue marked 'Mafeking 1900 Siege (Gen. Robert S. S. Baden-Powell)'

Vryburg
(a) Stamps issued in Vryburg under Boer Occupation (Vryburg was the capital of the Boer Republic 'Stellaland' from 1884 to 1885. Stellaland was annexed by Great Britain in 1885).
1884 – 1896 Cape of Good Hope stamps surcharged and marked 'Z.A.R':
    ½d. surcharge on ½d. emerald
    1d. surcharge on 1d. rose
    2d. surcharge on 6d. violet
    2½d. surcharge on 2½d. ultramarine

(b) Stamps issued in Vryburg under British Occupation.

1895 – 1896 Transvaal stamps marked 'V.R. Special Post':
    ½d. green
    1d. rose and green
    2d. brown and green
    2½d. ultramarine and green

Natal
Many of the Natal stamps issued prior to 1899 were still in use in Natal at the outbreak of the Boer War.

(a) Issue of 1882 – 1889 marked 'Natal Postage' (with Queen Victoria):
    ½d. blue-green
    ½d. grey green
    1d. rose
    3d. ultramarine
    3d. grey
    4d. brown
    6d. violet

(b) Issue of 1885 – 1886 Natal stamps with a surcharge:
    ½d. surcharge on 1d. rose
    2d. surcharge on 3d. grey

(c) Issue of 1887 marked 'Natal Postage' (with Queen Victoria):
    2d. olive-green
    1s. orange
    2½d. surcharged on 4d. brown

(d) Issue of 1891 marked 'Natal Postage' (with Queen Victoria):
    2½d. ultramarine
    ½d. surcharge on 6d. violet
    ½d. surcharge on 1d. rose

(e) Issue of 1902 – 1903 marked 'Postage-Natal-Revenue' (with King Edward VII):
    ½d. blue green
    1d. rose
    1½d. black and blue-green
    2d. olive-green and scarlet
    2½d. ultramarine
    3d. grey and red-violet
    4d. brown and scarlet
    5d. orange and black
    6d. maroon and blue-green

1s. pale blue and deep rose
2s. violet and blue-green
2s.6d. red-violet
4s. yellow and deep rose
5s. carmine lake and dark blue
10s. brown and deep rose
£1 ultramarine and black
£1–10s. violet and blue-green
£5 black and violet
£10 orange and green
£20 green and carmine

Orange Free State (Oranje Vrij Staat)
The Orange Free State Republic issued the following stamps.

(*a*) Issue of 1868–1900 marked 'Oranje Vrij Staat' (with Orange Tree):
$\frac{1}{2}$d. red-brown
$\frac{1}{2}$d. orange
1d. brown
1d. violet
2d. violet
3d. ultramarine
4d. ultramarine
6d. carmine-rose
1s. orange
1s. brown
5s. green

(*b*) There were a number of issues with surcharges:
1877 '4' surcharge on 6d. rose
1881 '1d.' surcharge on 5s. green
1882 '$\frac{1}{2}$d.' surcharge on 5s. green
1882 '3d.' surcharge on 4d. ultramarine
1888 '2d.' surcharge on 3d. ultramarine
1890–91 '1d.' surcharge on 3d.
1892 '2$\frac{1}{2}$d.' surcharge on 3d. ultramarine
1896 '$\frac{1}{2}$d.' surcharge on 3d. ultramarine
1896 'Halve penny' surcharge on 3d. ultramarine
1897 '2$\frac{1}{2}$d.' surcharge on 3d. ultramarine

Orange River Colony
After the capture of Bloemfontein, the capital of the Orange Free State Republic, the latter's name was changed to the Orange River Colony.

(*a*) Issue under British Occupation marked 'V.R.I.' (Victoria Regina Imperatrix) and surcharge on Orange Free State stamps:
1900
$\frac{1}{2}$d. surcharge on $\frac{1}{2}$d. orange
1d. surcharge on 1d. violet
1d. surcharge on 1d. brown
2d. surcharge on 2d. violet
2$\frac{1}{2}$d. surcharge on 3d. ultramarine
3d. surcharge on 3d. ultramarine
4d. surcharge on 4d. ultramarine
6d. surcharge on 6d. carmine-rose
6d. surcharge on 6d. ultramarine
1s. surcharge on 1s. brown
1s. surcharge on 1s. orange
5s. surcharge on 5s. green

The 1900–01 issues of the above stamps had the full points in 'V.R.I.' raised above the bottoms of the letters.

(*b*) The following Cape of Good Hope stamps of 1893–98 were overprinted 'Orange River Colony':
$\frac{1}{2}$d. green
2$\frac{1}{2}$d. ultramarine
1d. carmine-rose

(*c*) From 1902 a 'E.R.I.' (Edward Rex Imperator) overprint was also used, plus a surcharge:
4d. on 6d. on 6d. ultramarine
6d. on 6d. ultramarine
1s. on 5s. on 5s. green

(*d*) From 1903 Orange River Colony stamps were issued (with King Edward VII).

Swaziland
From 1894 to 1906 Swaziland was under outside administration, initially that of the South African Republic, and then that of the Transvaal Colony. Until 1895 the stamps in use were the South African Republic stamps (Z. Afr. Republiek) overprinted with 'Swaziland'.

South African Republic (Transvaal) (Z. Afr. Republiek)

(*a*) Issue of 1896 marked with the crest of the Republic:
$\frac{1}{2}$d. green

1d. rose and green
2d. brown and green
2½d. ultramarine and green
4d. olive and green
6d. violet and green
1s. bistre and green
2d. 6d. heliotrope and green
5s. slate-blue
10s. red-brown
£5 dark green

(*b*) Issue of 1901 printed in Pietersburg (in the field) with signature and '1901' at the bottom (imperforate and perforated stamps):
½d. green
1d. rose
2d. orange
4d. dull blue
6d. green
1s. yellow

Transvaal
The first Transvaal stamps were issued under military authority.

(*a*) Issue of 1900 were South African Republic stamps overprinted 'V.R.I.':
½d. to £5 stamps

(*b*) In 1900 there were surcharges together with 'V.R.I.' overprints:
3d. surcharge on 1d. rose and green
1d. surcharge on 1d. red
3d. surcharge on 1d. red

(*c*) Issue of 1900 (issued in Rustenburg) South African Republic stamps with 'V.R.I.' in violet handstamped overprint:
½d. to 2s. 6d. stamps

(*d*) Issue of 1900 (issued in Schweizer Reinecke) South African Republic stamps handstamped 'Besieged':
½d. to 6d. stamps

(*e*) Issue of 1900 (issued in Wolmaranstad) South African Republic stamps overprinted 'Cancelled' and 'V-R-I'.

(*f*) Issue of 1901–02 South African Republic stamps with overprint 'V.R.I.' and surcharged:
½d. surcharge on 2d. brown and green
½d. green
1d. rose and green
3d. red violet and green
4d. olive and green
2s. 6d. heliotrope and green

(*g*) Issue of 1902–03 marked 'Transvaal' (with King Edward VII):
½d. grey-green and black
1d. rose and black
2d. violet and black
2½d. ultramarine and black
3d. olive green and black
4d. chocolate and black
6d. brown-orange and black
1s. olive-green and black
1s. red-brown and black
2s. brown and black
2s. yellow and black
2s. 6d. black and violet
5s. violet, black, yellow
10s. violet, black, red
£1 violet and green
£5 violet and orange

Pietersburg Stamps
After Lord Roberts captured Pretoria, the capital of the South African Republic moved north to Pietersburg. When their Post Office ran out of ZAR stamps they minted new stamps called the 'Pietersburg Stamps'.

Ermelo and Carolina Stamps
In the later stages of the war the headquarters of the South African Republican Forces were moved to the Eastern Transvaal. Here they created a mail service which was called the *Oos-Hoëveldse Posdiens* (East Highveld Postal Service). As there were no printing presses they typed their new stamps and these stamps are now known as the 'Ermelo and Carolina Stamps'.

BOER WAR COVERS
There is great interest in the collection of Boer War covers, which carry many different stamps, postmarks, censor marks and marks of the POW camps, and were mailed from the

war zones in South Africa to the rest of the world.

Many collectors are interested in Boer War envelopes irrespective of the marks and the stamps on the covers. Mail from the besieged towns of Kimberley, Mafeking and Ladysmith generates a great deal of interest. The most popular collectors' items are probably the covers from besieged Mafeking, where special stamps were issued under the command of Baden-Powell. The stamps of the Cape of Good Hope and the Bechuanaland Protectorate were also used and overstamped 'Mafeking Besieged'.

Prisoner-of-War Covers
In 1902 at the end of the Boer War there were 30,000 prisoners of war in POW camps in South Africa and overseas. Because of the widespread dispersal of the camps and the diversity of the nationalities of the POWs — Boers, Dutch, Irish, Germans and Huguenot Settlers — the collection of POW mail became very popular. There was also a great volume of mail. From the camps in St. Helena alone 16,000 items per month were being posted by the end of the war.

Many collectors specialise in certain aspects of the POW mail — for example, endeavouring to collect covers addressed to and from all the POW camps. There were camps at the following locations:

In South Africa
Belle Vue at Simonstown in the Cape Colony
Green Point, near Cape Town
Ladysmith (Tin Town Camp) in Natal
Merebank near Durban in Natal
Montrose near Durban
Umbilo in Durban
Pretoria in the Transvaal Colony
In addition, the following transport ships were used as temporary prisoner-of-war camps:
S.S. *Armenian Castle*
Catalonia
City of Cambridge
Harwarden Castle
Kildonan Castle
Manilla
Manlate
Mongolian
Orient
Penelope
Pindoure
Ranee
Yorkshire

In Bermuda
Burt's Island
Darrell's Island
Hawkins' Island
Hinson's Island (also called Godet Island)
Long Island
Morgan's Island
Port Island
Smith's Island
Tucker's Island

In British West Indies
Dominica

In St. Helena
Broad Bottom
Deadwood Camp
Deadwood No. 2 Camp
Fort High Knoll
Jamestown

In Ceylon
Diyatalawa
Ragama
Urugasmanhandiya
Mount Lavinia
Hambantota

In India
Abbottabad
Ahmednagar
Bellary
Bhim Tal
Dagshai
Fort Govindgarh (also called Amritsar)
Kaity
Kakool
Nilgiri
Satara
Shahjahanpur
Sialkot
Solon
Trichinopoly
Umballa
Upper Topa (also called Murree Hills)
Wellington

The mail to the POWs usually carries one of the following marks:
P.O.W. *or*
P. of W. *or*
Krijgsgevangene (P.O.W.) *or*
Botenschamp.

Mail from the POWs usually has the stamps of the countries the camps were located in.

The rarest covers to find are those addressed to and from the British prisoners of war in the Boer-controlled camps. The biggest camps were in Pretoria, the capital of the South African Republic, and in Bloemfontein, the capital of the Orange Free State Republic.

POSTMARKS AND CENSOR'S SEALS

Ordinary mail from South Africa during the period 1899-1902 with censor or martial law marks is also being collected as Boer War memorabilia. Some collectors specialise in the collection of Army or Field Post Office marks or censors' seals and marks. The stamps of the British Army Post Offices (Field Post Offices) are popular. The Army Post Offices stayed on the railway lines. Later, during the guerilla war stage, the Post Offices settled down in the towns where they were located.

After the Boer Forces invaded and occupied part of Natal, their Field Post Offices used their own stamps (ZAR and OVS stamps) with a '*Veldpost*' (Field Post) cancellation and the name of the town in the Colony of Natal. In some instances they used the unchanged stamp of the town they were occupying to cancel their own stamps.

RED CROSS MAIL

A number of collectors are interested in 'Red Cross' covers and letters. This is also an extensive field to cover as there are Red Cross Societies in most countries and there were a number of Red Cross Societies in South Africa. Not many of the covers have survived, and consequently Red Cross covers have become very rare. However, they do turn up at auctions occasionally, but their prices are rising steadily.

Stamps and Covers

Plate 121
A few examples of:
(*a*) Cape of Good Hope postage stamps;
(*b*) Natal postage stamps;
(*c*) Orange Free State postage stamps overprinted 'V.R.I.' and the amount;
(*d*) Cape of Good Hope postage stamps overprinted 'Orange River Colony'.
(*From the Oosthuizen Collection*)

72 Boer War Memorabilia

Plate 122
A number of examples of:
(*a*) ZAR (*Zuid-Afrikaansche Republiek*—South African Republic or Transvaal) postage stamps;
(*b*) ZAR postage stamps overprinted with 'E.R.I.' and 'E.R.I.' plus an amount;
(*c*) ZAR postage stamps overprinted with 'V.R.I.'
(*From the Oosthuizen Collection*)

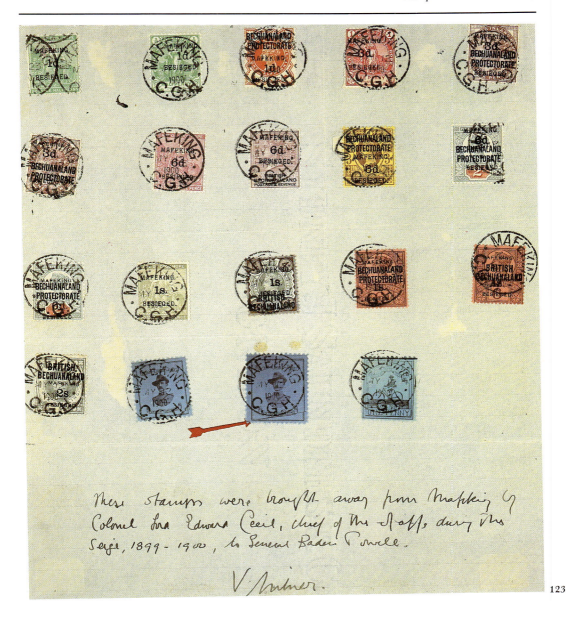

Plate 123
A very interesting collection of the various stamps which were in use in Mafeking during the Siege of Mafeking, including the 'Mafeking Stamps'. The footnote on the page reads: 'These stamps were brought away from Mafeking by Colonel Lord Edward Cecil, Chief of Staff, during the Siege, 1899–1900 to General Baden-Powell'.
(*Photograph by courtesy of Sotheby's, London*)

74   Boer War Memorabilia

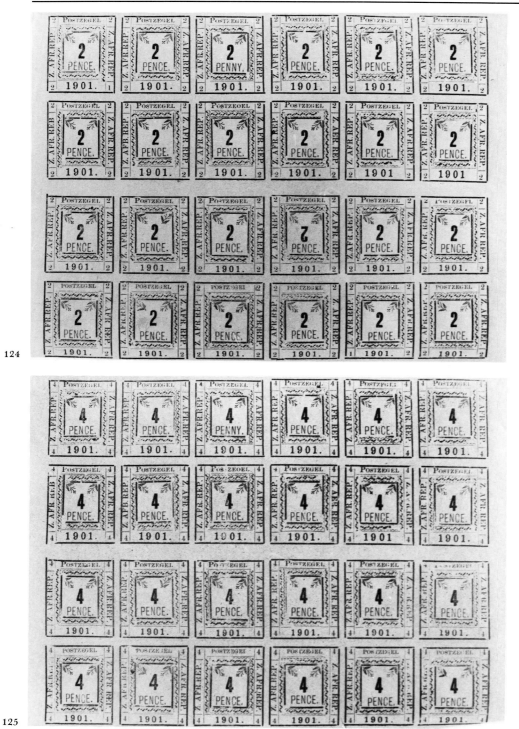

124

125

Stamps and Covers 75

Plate 124
A sheet of South African Republic '2 pence' stamps printed in Pietersburg in 1901.
(*By courtesy of the National Cultural History and Open-Air Museum, Pretoria*)

Plate 125
A sheet of South African Republic '4 pence' stamps printed in Pietersburg in 1901.
(*By courtesy of the National Cultural History and Open-Air Museum, Pretoria*)

Plate 127
Two covers with the field stamps issued in the Orange Free State during the War. The stamps are imprinted 'Commando Brief/O.V.S./Franko'.
(*By courtesy of the War Museum of the Boer Republics, Bloemfontein*)

Plate 126
Four examples of the 'Ermelo and Carolina' stamps issued by the South African Republic on the Eastern Highveld from March to June 1901. These are the fourpence, sixpence, one shilling and one penny denominations.
(*By courtesy of the War Museum of the Boer Republics, Bloemfontein*)

Plate 128

Row 1
Envelope 1: (*a*) An envelope with a Transvaal stamp cancelled by the Pretoria Post Office addressed to a POW on Hawkin's Island, Bermuda.
(*b*) Stamped: Passed Press Censor, Pretoria.

Envelope 2: (*a*) An envelope with a Cape of Good Hope stamp with a Cape Town Post Office cancellation.
(*b*) A paper seal marked: Opened under Martial Law.
(*c*) Stamped: Passed Press Censor, Cape Town.

Boer War Memorabilia

Row 2
Envelope 1: (*a*) Envelope with a Cape of Good Hope stamp and a Beaconsfield Post Office cancellation.
(*b*) A paper seal marked: Opened under Martial Law.
(*c*) Stamped: Passed Press Censor, Port Elizabeth.
(*d*) Port Elizabeth Post Office cancellation.
(*e*) Stamped: Passed Censor, Beaconsfield.

Envelope 2: (*a*) An envelope with an Orange Free State 'V.R.I.' stamp cancelled by the Heilbron Post Office.
(*b*) Stamped: Passed Censor.
(*c*) Stamped: P.B.C.
(*d*) Addressed to a POW in Deadwood Camp No. 2, St. Helena.

Row 3
Envelope 1: (*a*) A postcard from the Diyatalawa Camp carrying a Ceylon stamp with a Ceylon Post Office cancellation.
(*b*) Stamped: Passed by Censors, Diyatalawa Camp.
(*c*) Stamped: Passed Press Censor, Johannesburg.
(*d*) Postal cancellation, Pretoria, Transvaal.

Envelope 2: (*a*) A POW letter with a Ceylon stamp with a Diyatalawa Camp Post Office cancellation, addressed to a POW in Tin Town Camp, Ladysmith.
(*b*) Stamped: Passed Censor, Diyatalawa Camp.

Row 4
Envelope 1: (a) An envelope with a ZAR stamp overstamped 'E.R.I.' and cancelled by the Pretoria Post Office, addressed to a POW in Bermuda.
(*b*) Stamped: Passed Press Censor, Pretoria.

Envelope 2: (*a*) An envelope with a Cape of Good Hope stamp cancelled in Cape Town.
(*b*) Pink paper seal (on back) marked: Opened under Martial Law.
(*c*) On the back a Durban and Colombo Post Office cancellation.
(*d*) Stamped: Passed Censor Diyatalawa Camp.

Plate 129
An envelope with the crest of The Devonshire Regiment, addressed to a British prisoner of war in the Boer POW Camp in Pretoria. The envelope carries the following.
(*a*) An English stamp with the cancellation of the 'Field Post Office – British Army S. Africa'.
(*b*) A triangular rubber stamp 'Passed/ Press/Censor'.
(*c*) An oval stamp 'Consulate of the United States of America to the S.A.R. Pretoria'. The US Consulate assumed diplomatic responsibility for the British POWs.
(*d*) A round stamp *Ontvangen* 30/4/00' (received).
(*e*) A round Boer censor stamp '*Gezien* 2 Mei 1900' (Censor).
(*By courtesy of the War Museum of the Boer Republics, Bloemfontein*)

Plate 130

Figure 1: Unused South African Republic postcard printed by the government press in the field, Machadodorp, ZAR (Eastern Transvaal).

Figure 2: South African Republic (Transvaal) postcard. The card carries a 1d. ZAR stamp overstamped 'V.R.I.' cancelled by the Pretoria Post Office and also stamped 'Passed Press Censor, Pretoria'.
(*Both from the Oosthuizen Collection*)

Boer War Memorabilia

130

Stamps and Covers

131

132

Plate 131

Left page: The cover carries two English 'One Penny' stamps. The Cape of Good Hope Post Office at De Aar stamped the letter but was not permitted to cancel the English stamps. The cover was then forwarded to a British Army Field Post Office where the stamps were cancelled. There is also a pencilled tax mark on the envelope. The picture below is of a hospital camp in De Aar.

Right page: This cover addressed to 'Capt the Earl of Cardigan' carries a English 'One Penny' stamp overstamped 'Army Official' and cancelled by the 'Ladysmith Siege Post Office' on 27th February 1900 (one day before the Relief of Ladysmith). The picture above the cover is of Sir George White's headquarters at Ladysmith, showing the shell-proof shelter.
(*From the collection of Mr Kenneth Griffith, London*)

Plate 132

Top cover: A cover of the British Red Cross Society, South Africa, Natal Branch. No stamp but with a Durban Post Office cancellation.

Left bottom cover: A cover of the '*Vereeniging het Roode Kruis van Geneve, Hoofdbestuur der Transvaalsche Afdeling*' (Red Cross Society of Geneva, Management of the Transvaal Division).

Right bottom cover: A cover from a Dutch Ambulance unit in Natal marked: '*Ambulance, Nederlandsche Roode Kruis*' (Dutch Red Cross). The cover carries a 2½d. stamp of the South African Republic with an 'Elandslaagte 8 Feb 1900' cancellation. (The Battle of Elandslaagte took place on 21st October 1899.)
(*From the collection of Mr Kenneth Griffith, London*)

Plate 133

There was a shortage of paper in the Transvaal during the war. After the capture of Pretoria Lord Kitchener used the stationery of the Transvaal Red Cross Society for his personal notes. This note was addressed to 'Captain Little' (*see* Plate) reading:

O.H.M.S.
ULTIMATUM
If this tent is not evacuated
in three minutes after receipt
of this order it will be shelled.
by order
K of K
(Kitchener of Khartoum)

(*From the collection of Mr Kenneth Griffith, London*)

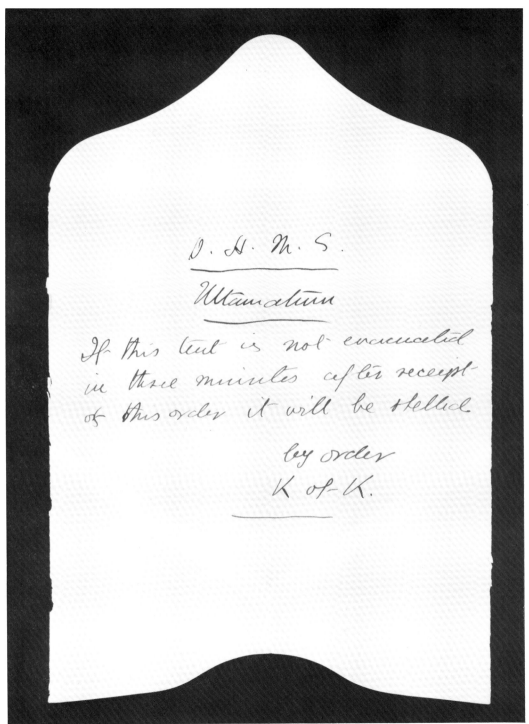

133

CHAPTER 6

Prisoner-of-War Handicraft

Wood, bone, horn and ivory items and carvings, pipes, textiles, metal items and stone carvings

During the period 1900 to 1902 a great number of Boer prisoners of war were shipped to overseas camps. Transport ships were converted into prison-ships and used as collection centres before the prisoners were shipped to overseas camps. These prison-ships were eventually abandoned and POW camps established at Green Point near Cape Town, Belle Vue at Simonstown in the Cape Colony, Tin Town Camp in Ladysmith in Natal, in and around Durban at Merebank, Montrose and Umbilo and at Pretoria in the Transvaal Colony. There was also a hospital camp at Jacobsdal.

In April 1900 the first POW camp was established on the island of St. Helena at Deadwood. Later more camps were established on St. Helena at Deadwood, Camp No. 2, Broadbottom, Fort High Knoll and Jamestown.

The greatest number of POWs were shipped to Bermuda, where a number of camps were established on different islands, namely Burt's Island, Darrell's Island, Hawkin's Island, Hinson's Island (also called Godet Island), Long Island, Morgan's Island, Port Island, Smith's Island and Tucker's Island.

There is also evidence that there was a camp in Dominica in the British West Indies.

In Sri Lanka (Ceylon) there were three main POW camps, at Diyatalawa (also called Happy Valley), Ragama and Mount Lavinia. Later camps were established at Urugasmanhandiya and Hambantota.

In India a great number of camps were established, but only a small number of prisoners were placed in each camp. The best-known camp was the Commandani Camp at Trichinopoly. The other camps were at Abbottabad, Ahmednagar, Bellary, Bhim Tal, Dagshai, Fort Govindgarh (also called Amritsar) Kaity, Kakool, Nilgiri, Satara, Shahjahanpur, Sailkot, Solon, Umballa, Upper Topa (also called Murree Hills) and Wellington.

At the end of the war there were 24,000 prisoners of war in the overseas camps and 6,000 in camps in South Africa.

To earn more pocket money to supplement their diet or to buy tobacco, or simply to relieve their boredom, the prisoners turned to making curios, carving toys and many different kinds of artifacts. As tools were scarce the pocket knives of the POWs became the most commonly used tool. For material they used wood, bone, ivory, stone, horn and textiles.

Apart from some beautifully detailed models, the prisoners, in their efforts to make money, mass-produced the following: walking sticks, pens, trick boxes, needle holders, tobacco jars, horn cups, serviette rings, paper knives, stone crests, embroidered handkerchiefs, brooches and toys.

The POWs in the Burt's Island camp created an 'Industrial Association for Carvings and Curios' which enabled their work to be sold through many stores in Bermuda. In Bermuda the Women's Work Exchange organized weekly sales in the camps and also sold some of the handicrafts at their offices in Hamilton. A great amount of the Bermuda POW handicrafts found its way into the United States. Recently a substantial supply of handicraft was discovered in the attic of a house in Bermuda, which was occupied by one of the ladies of the Women's Work Exchange at the turn of the century.

It is common for the handiwork to have been marked with 'POW' signs, sometimes with a date, or with the name of the camp, or the country it was located in e.g. 'Ceylon', and in many cases with the names of the prisoners. However, a great number of items were produced without any markings. Items were also marked by the members of the prisoners' families who received the items as gifts or heirlooms. A number of the items were marked in ink.

Handicrafts were also made by the internees in the internment camps. In the later stages of the war the Boer women, children and old people were interned in camps. These internment camps later became known as concentration camps. There were fifty concentration camps in the Transvaal Colony and in the Orange River Colony. A great number of items were made in these camps and they are also being collected.

During the latter stage of the war a number of Boers crossed over into Mozambique. The British authorities in the Transvaal considered them a potential threat and at the request of the British Government the Portuguese Government moved the Boers from Mozambique into internment camps in Portugal. The best-known camp was in Peniche.

134

Plate 134

A coach carved from bone drawn by horses carved out of wood.
On the back seat, inside the coach, a small carved figure of President Kruger.
On the door of the coach the South African Republic Emblem, the words '*Eendracht maakt magt*' (unity is strength) and the inscription: 'I. Ebersohn, Darrells Eiland, Bermuda 1902'.
(12 in. – 30.5 cm. long: 4 in. – 10.2 cm. high)
(*By courtesy of the War Museum of the Boer Republics, Bloemfontein*)

Plates 135 and 136

An ox-cart made by a Boer prisoner of war, marked
'Commandari Boer Camp, Trichy'.

Plate 135: A front view of the ox-cart.

Plate 136: Rear view of the ox-cart.
(*By courtesy of Major Philip Erskine, Stellenbosch*)

Plate 137

A large model of an ox-wagon with carved oxen made by a prisoner of war.
(*By permission of the National Army Museum, London*)

Plate 138
A miniature doll's settee carved by a Boer POW on St. Helena.
(*By permission of the Africana Museum, Johannesburg*)

Plate 139
Treen made by prisoners of war.

Top row
Figure 1: Small box with the inscription 'St. Helena — P.O.W. 1901'.
($2\frac{5}{8}$ in. – 6.7 cm.)

Figure 2: Box with trick opening with the inscription 'A. Schneider — P.O.W. — Morgans Isle'.
($3\frac{5}{8} \times 1\frac{3}{4}$ in. – 9.2 × 4.5 cm.)

Figure 3: Trick box with a snake (based on the seventeenth century tombstone snuff boxes) with the inscription 'Made by a P.O.W. St. Helena, W. Loxley'.
($3\frac{1}{4}$ in. – 8.3 cm.)

Figure 4: Tobacco jar with the inlay reading 'Souvenir'.
($6\frac{3}{4}$ in. – 17.2 cm.)

Figure 5: A small shoe trick-box with the inscriptions 'Upper Topa 1902' and 'By a Boer Prisoner of War'.
($4\frac{1}{4}$ in. – 10.8 cm.)

Figure 6: Round trick-box with a snake (tombstone model). Maker's name in faded ink.
(4 in. – 10.2 cm.)

Centre row
Figure 1: A small trick shoe with the inscription, 'P.O.W. St. Helena'.
($3\frac{1}{2}$ in. – 9 cm.)

Figure 2: Needle-box with the inscription, 'Made by P.O.W. St. Helena 1901'.
(3 in. – 7.5 cm.)

Figure 3: Serviette ring with the inscription 'St. Helena, 7.8 1901'.
($1\frac{3}{4}$ in. – 4.5 cm.)

Figure 4: Trick shoe with a snake. Unmarked.
($5\frac{1}{2}$ in. – 14 cm.)
(*All from the Oosthuizen Collection*)

Bottom figure: A carved gun with the inscription 'Prisoner of War, Feb 27 1900. St. Helena 1901'.
(*From the collection of Mr Kenneth Griffith, London*)

140

Plate 140
Carved walking sticks.

Figure 1: With carved horse's hoof handle inscribed 'H. D. Naude P.O.W. 1902 Hawkins'.

Figure 2: With carved horse's head handle inscribed 'B. B. Bruce St. H P.O.W. 1901'.

Figure 3: With a carved lion inscribed 'Made by a P.O.W. St. Helena 1901'.

Figure 4: With a carved head of a gentleman inscribed 'Made by P.O.W. St. Helena 1901'.

Figure 5: With a panel showing a Boer carrying a gun. Unmarked.

Figure 6: With a carved horn handle with the inscription 'P.O.W. St. Helena 1901'.
(*All from the collection of Mr Kenneth Griffith, London*)

Plates 141 and 142
A folding chair. On the top cross-slat of the chair the inscription 'S. Y. Crouse P.O.W. Darrell's Isle Bermuda 1902'.
(*By courtesy of Mr Lawrence Mills, Bermuda; photographs by Lloyd Webbe*)

141

142

143

144

Plate 143
A wooden bottle with a leopard carved on one side and a lion on the other.
(*By courtesy of the National Cultural History and Open-Air Museum, Pretoria*)

Plate 144
A carved coconut with silver trimmings on a silver stand. On the front the Transvaal coat-of-arms and the inscription: 'J. D. Petersen, Ahmednagar Fort, India 1902'.
(8 in. – 20.3 cm.)
(*By courtesy of the National Cultural History and Open-Air Museum, Pretoria*)

Plate 145
A puzzle game made out of wood by a prisoner of war.
(*By courtesy of the National Cultural History and Open-Air Museum, Pretoria*)

Plate 146
Figure 1: Articulated wooden toy chameleon inscribed 'F. A. Venter, Krygsgevangener Paardenberg' and a red Censor's stamp 'Bellevue'. ($4\frac{15}{16}$ in. – 12.5 cm.)

Prisoner-of-War Handicraft   89

145

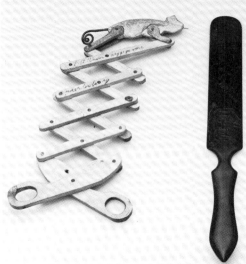

146

147

148

Figure 2: A carved wooden paper-knife with the coats-of-arms of the South African Republic and the Orange Free State Republic and inscribed 'Lord Roberts occupied Pretoria Z.A.R. 5th June 1900' and 'Made in Boer Camp J.C.R.P. of W. 1900 Ceylon 1902'.   ($13\frac{3}{4}$ in. – 35 cm.)
(*Both by courtesy of Sotheby's, Johannesburg*)

Plate 147
A squirrel carved by a prisoner of war. No inscription.
(*By permission of the National Army Museum, London*)

Plate 148
A Bermuda cedar picture frame inscribed 'Made by W. M. Du Plooi P.O.W. Hinsons Island Bermuda 1902'.
Watercolour of the coat-of-arms of the South African Republic painted by POW Mader.
(15 × 12 in. – 38.1 × 30.5 cm.)
(*From the collection of Sup. A. P. Bermingham, Bermuda*)

Plate 149
A picture frame with attractive inlays and the words '*Aus meiner Kriegsgefangenschaft*' (from my internment): made by L. Zimmerer.
(*By courtesy of the National Cultural History and Open-Air Museum, Pretoria*)

Figure 2: A simple Bermuda cedar candlestick.
(8 in. – 20.3 cm. high: 4 in. – 10.2 cm. wide.)
(*From the collection of Sup. A. P. Bermingham, Bermuda*)

Plate 151
An unusual trick-box with two snakes.
(*From the Benbow Collection, Bermuda*)

Plate 150

Figure 1: An ornate candlestick made from mahogany inscribed 'Bermuda'.
(9 in. – 22.8 cm. long: 5 in. – 12.7 cm. wide)

Plate 152

Figure 1: A carved wooden paperweight with the coat-of-arms of the ZAR (South African Republic) with the motto: '*Eendracht maakt magt*' (unity is strength). On the sides the inscription: 'Boeren Kamp' and 'Ceylon 1902'.
($3\frac{1}{4}$ in. – 8.2 cm.)

Figure 2: A carved stone bible with the inscription: '*Boeren Oorlog*' (Boer War) and '1899 – 1902'.
($2\frac{1}{4}$ in. – 5.7 cm.)

Figure 3: A pair of carved stone medallions, the first of Queen Victoria, the second of

President Kruger. On the back of each medallion the inscription 'Made by Boer Prisoner of War St. Helena 8/7/1901'.
(*All from the Oosthuizen Collection*)

Plate 153
A plough made from Bermuda cedar inscribed: 'Bermuda 1902'.
(10 in. – 25.4 cm. long: 6 in. – 15.2 cm. hgh)
(*From the collection of Sup. A. P. Bermingham, Bermuda*)

Plate 154

Figure 1: A paper-knife with a bone blade and a wooden handle inscribed 'Boer Kamp Ceylon — 1901'. ($7\frac{1}{2}$ in. – 19 cm.)

Figure 2: A horn cup inscribed 'Boer Camp Ceylon 1902 — Freedom — Patience — Courage' and bearing the coat-of-arms of the South African Republic. ($4\frac{1}{4}$ in. – 10.5 cm.)

Figure 3: A horn cup inscribed 'Van Tim Holloway aan W. J. DeKock Krygsgevangenen Juni 1901 Diyatalawa Camp Ceylon'. ($3\frac{1}{2}$ in. – 8.9 cm.)

Figure 4: A bone box. On the lid the inscription: 'Boer War 1899–1901'. ($1\frac{3}{4}$ in. – 4.5 cm.)

(*Figure 3 from the collection of Mr Kenneth Griffith, London; the other items from the Oosthuizen Collection*)

Plate 155

A stone inkwell in the form of a tortoise. The lid of the inkwell in the form of Lord Kitchener's head with the figures '1899–1902' on the hat. (3 in. – 7.6 cm.)
(*By courtesy of the War Museum of the Boer Republics, Bloemfontein*)

Plate 156

A photograph of prisoners of war belonging to the Burt's Island Industrial Association displaying their wares.
(*Photograph from the De Villiers Album, Durban; kindly supplied by Mr Colin Benbow, Bermuda*)

Plate 157

Three examples of egg-cups on stands made by Boer prisoners of war in the POW camps.
(*By courtesy of the War Museum of the Boer Republics, Bloemfontein*)

156

157

94 Boer War Memorabilia

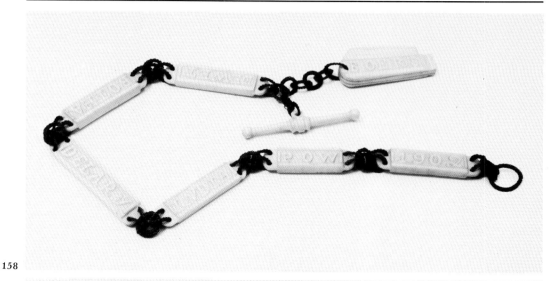

158

159

Plate 158
A bone watch-chain with a bone knife. The links have been engraved as follows: 'Boers — De Wet — Botha — Delary — India — P.O.W. — 1902'.
(*By permission of the National Army Museum, London*)

Plate 159
A card from Ceylon dated 1901, with a carved bone watch-chain, a bone brooch and wooden buttons with bone inlays.
(*By courtesy of the National Cultural History and Open-Air Museum, Pretoria*)

Prisoner-of-War Handicraft   95

Plate 160
Three enamelled metal plates with various coats-of-arms.
(*By permission of the Africana Museum, Johannesburg*)

Plate 161

Figure 1: A beefbone wristband (or serviette ring).   (3½ in. – 8.9 cm.)

Figure 2: Beefbone brooch inscribed 'Burtts Bermuda'.   (1½ in. – 3.8 cm.)
(*From the collection of Sup. A. P. Bermingham, Bermuda*)

Plate 162
A bone serviette ring engraved with the Transvaal coat-of-arms and the words 'Souvenir St. Helena 1901'.
(*By courtesy of the National Cultural History and Open-Air Museum, Pretoria*)

Plate 163
A woollen checkerboard with bone counters, made by a POW.
(*By permission of the National Army Museum, London*)

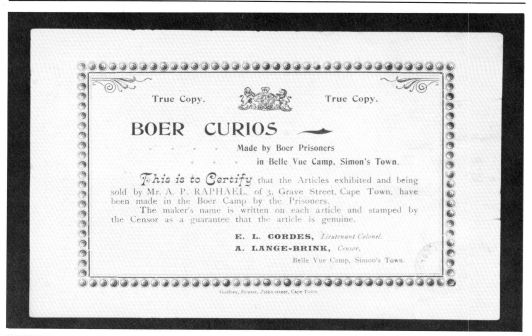

164

165

Prisoner-of-War Handicraft 97

Plate 164
A certificate reading:
'True Copy. Boer Curios. Made by Boer Prisoners in the Belle Vue Camp, Simon's Town. This is to certify that the Articles exhibited and being sold by Mr. A. P. Raphael, of 3, Grave Street, Cape Town, have been made in the Boer Camp by the Prisoners. The maker's name is written on each article and stamped by the Censor as guarantee that the article is genuine.
E. L. Cordes Lieutenant Colonel.
A. Lange-Brink Censor
Belle Vue Camp, Simon's Town'.

Stamped with a round censor's stamp.
$(8\frac{1}{4} \times 5\frac{1}{4}$ in. $- 21 \times 13.4$ cm.$)$
(*From the collection of Mr Kenneth Griffith, London*)

Plate 165
Coin cut-outs and engraving on coins from the POW camps.
Top row
Figure 1: A ZAR (South African Republic) 1s. cut-out with a crown and pipe added.

Figure 2: A ZAR 6d. as a pendant.
Middle row
Figure 3: A cut-out 2s. piece as a pendant.
Figure 4: A copper 1d. ZAR coin as pendant with a silver hat and pipe added.
Figure 5: A silver 2s. coin cut-out with a hat and pipe added.

Bottom row
Figure 6: A ZAR 1s. with a hat engraved on President Kruger.
Figure 7: A silver 1s. ZAR coin with a hat and pipe engraved on the figure of President Kruger.
(*From the Oosthuizen Collection*)

Textiles made by the Prisoners of War in the Overseas Camps

Plate 166
A hat band embroidered with the Transvaal and Orange Free State flags and the words '*Voor Vryheid en Recht*' (for freedom and right).
(*By courtesy of the National Cultural History and Open-Air Museum, Pretoria*)

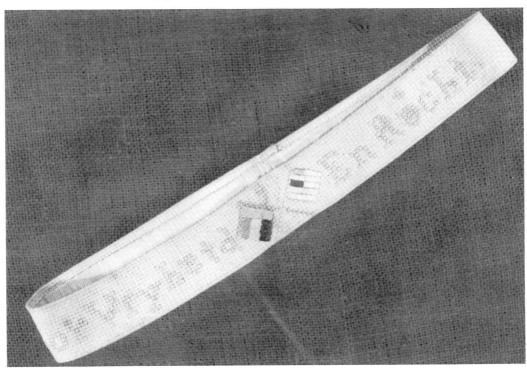

166

98 Boer War Memorabilia

Plate 167
A crocheted neck tie.
(*By courtesy of the National Cultural History and Open-Air Museum, Pretoria*)

Plate 168
A woven neck tie.
(*By courtesy of the National Cultural History and Open-Air Museum, Pretoria*)

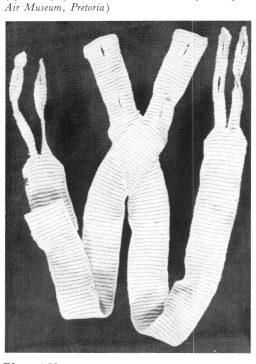

Plate 169
A crocheted pair of braces.
(*By courtesy of the National Cultural History and Open-Air Museum, Pretoria*)

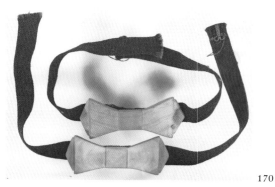

Plate 170
A pair of bow-ties, with woven bands and carved wooden bows.
By courtesy of the National Cultural History and Open-Air Museum, Pretoria)

Prisoner-of-War Handicraft 99

Plate 171
A photograph of two prisoners of war sitting outside their tent in a POW camp, working on a cloth.
(*By courtesy of the National Cultural History and Open-Air Museum, Pretoria*)

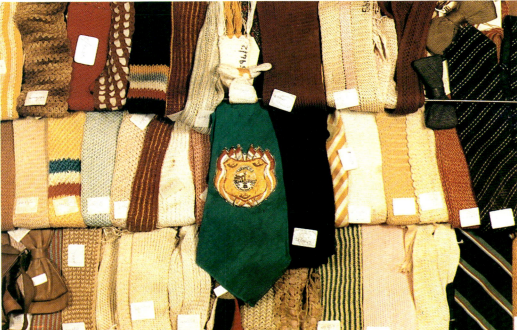

Plate 172
A collection of ties and bow-ties made by Boer prisoners of war in a POW camp.
(*By courtesy of the War Museum of the Boer Republics, Bloemfonein*)

CHAPTER 7

Coins and Notes

The hundreds of thousands in the field forces assigned to South Africa during the Boer War, all the Medical Staff and all those who visited South Africa during the war found it very easy to take home as a souvenir a coin of one of the Colonies and the South African Republic (ZAR — Zuid-Afrikaansche Republiek) and the Orange Free State (Oranje Vrijstaat). Almost every soldier returned to his home base with a ZAR coin bearing the face of President Kruger. Those who could afford it returned home with a gold coin or two in their pockets. Many of these gold and silver coins were turned into jewellery — brooches, pendants, rings, etc. — or were inserted in ashtrays or other ornaments as keepsakes.

Of all the Boer War memorabilia, coins and stamps are most probably still the easiest to find and buy in today's markets.

COINAGE
The most common coinage in use during the Boer War were as follows.

South African Republic ('Z.A.R.')

(*a*) *Gold coinage*
One Pound: 1892–1898 and 1900. (The 1892 was also issued with a double shaft on the ox-wagon.)
Blank rimless pound: 1900.
Blank pound with rim: 1900.
Veldpond (Field pound): 1902.
Half-pound: 1892–1897. (The 1892 coin was also issued with a double shaft on the ox-wagon.)
Blank half-pound with a rim: 1900.
Gold 3d.: 1898 (special issue).

(*b*) *Silver coinage*
5s. Crown: 1892 (with double and single shaft ox-wagon).
2s.6d.: 1892–1897.
Blank rimless 2s.6d.: 1900.
2s.: 1892–1897.
1s.: 1892–1897.
6d.: 1892–1897.
Blank 6d. with rim: 1900.
3d.: 1892–1897.
Blank 3d. with rim: 1900.

(*c*) *Copper coinage*
1d.: 1892–1894 and 1898.
Blank 1d. with rim: 1900.

Orange Free State Republic (Oranje Vrijstaat)
(a) *Silver coinage*
5s. Crown: 1887.
(b) *One penny (1d.)*
1874 bronze.
1888 in silver, bronze, nickel and aluminium.

Cape of Good Hope Colony
(a) *Silver coinage*
2s.6d.: 1889.
(b) *One penny (1d.)*
1889 in bronze, nickel, tin and aluminium.

Griquatown Coinage
One penny: 1890 in Bronze and Nickel. These were the only coins issued for Griquatown in the period close to the Boer War.

NOTES AND OTHER FORMS OF CURRENCY

Notes of the South African African Republic ('Z.A.R.')

(a) *Bank notes.* At the outbreak of the Boer War the following notes of *De Nationale Bank der Zuid-Afrikaansche Republiek* (the National Bank of the South African Republic) were in circulation:
£1 black-blue
£5 black-pink
£10 black-green
£20 black-pink
£50 black-mauve
£100 black-yellow

(b) *Government notes.* Because of difficulties with the British-controlled Banks, the Government was forced to issue their own notes backed by fixed property of the State. These notes were called *Gouvernements Noten* and £1, £5, £10, £20, £50 and £100 denominations were issued. All were dated 28th May 1900.

(c) *Pietersburg notes.* After the fall of Pretoria the seat of the Government was moved to Pietersburg. Here the same denominations in notes were issued, more crudely printed on stationery paper. The £1 and £5 notes were dated 1st February 1901, 1st March 1901 and 1st April 1901. The higher denominations were all dated 1st April 1901.

(d) *Pilgrims Rest or Field Notes (Te Velde).* The final series of ZAR notes were issued in the Eastern Transvaal at Pilgrims Rest. They are known as the *Te Velde* (field) notes. These notes were very crude and were printed on a small portable press on school notebook paper. Only £1, £5 and £10 notes were issued, the £5 and £10 on 1st March, 1st April and 1st May 1902, and the £1 on 1st May 1902.

Postal Orders
During the war blank postal order forms of the Transvaal and the Orange Free State circulated as currency. Both Republics issued postal orders in denominations of 1s., 2s.6d., 5s., 7s.6d., 10s., 12s.6d., 15s., 17s.6d. and £1.

Private Banks
The private banks in the Cape, Natal, Transvaal and Orange Free State issued their own notes during the period of the war.

Mafeking Siege Notes
During the Siege of Mafeking notes were issued by Colonel Baden-Powell with the aid of Mr R. Urry, Manager of the Standard Bank. The following notes were issued:
1s. green
2s. brown
3s. red
10s. in green ink
£1 blue
All the notes bore a one-penny embossed stamp of the Bechuanaland Protectorate.

Upington Border Scout Cloth 'Good Fors'
These highly-sought-after items were issued for army pay just before the end of the war. They were handwritten on different types of cloth and handsigned by Major Birkbeck O.C. They were issued in the following denominations: 2s., 5s., 10s., £1 and £2.

Prisoner of War Camp 'Good Fors'
Various prisoner-of war camps inside and outside South Africa issued 'good fors' to be

Coins and Notes 103

used to buy commodities, and they were used as currency in the camps. Tickets were issued to purchase soup, bread, coffee, etc. In South Africa the Green Point Camp issued 1s., 2s., 5s., 10s. and £1 'good fors', while at the Belle Vue Camp 6d. 1s., 2s., 5s. and 10s. 'good fors' were issued.

Miscellaneous
Various other siege money and 'good fors' were issued, e.g.:
Siege of Koffyfontein: £5;
Siege of Kimberley Soup Tickets: 6d.;
Mafeking Garrison Sowen (porridge) Ticket;
Siege of Mafeking Soup Ticket.

Plate 173
A picture of a Zuid-Afrikaansche Republiek (South African Republic) 1 *Pond* (one pound) gold coin and a ½ *Pond* (½ pound) gold coin.
(*From the Oosthuizen Collection*)

Plate 174
Examples of the silver and copper coinage of the Zuid-Afrikaansche Republiek (South African Republic).

5 shillings	1 shilling
2½ shillings	6 pence
2 shillings	3 pence
	1 penny.

(*From the Oosthuizen Collection*)

Plate 175

Figure 1: An 1888 copper 1 penny of the Oranje Vryjstaat (Orange Free State).

Figure 2: An 1890 copper 1 penny of the Zuid-Afrikaansche Republiek (South African Republic).
(*From the Oosthuizen Collection*)

Plates 176 and 177
The gold ZAR (Suid-Afrikaansche Republiek — South African Republic) *Een Pond* (one pound) coin made in the field. Commonly called the *Veldpond*.
(*Photography by Gerald Hoberman, Cape Town*)

Plates 178 and 179
The gold 3d. piece. This coin was minted at the request of President Kruger's friend Mr Sammy Marks.
(*Photography by Gerald Hoberman, Cape Town*)

Plate 180
Oranje Vryjstaat (Orange Free State) silver 1 *Kroon* (one crown).
(*Photography by Gerald Hoberman, Cape Town*)

Plate 181
Two examples of Cape of Good Hope 1 penny pieces.
(*Photography by Gerald Hoberman, Cape Town*)

Coins and Notes

Plate 182
Mafeking Siege Money: 1s., 2s., 3s., 10s. and £1.
(*By permission of the National Army Museum, London*)

Plate 183
A Mafeking one pound note dated March 1900.
(*Photograph by courtesy of Sotheby's, London*)

Plate 184
Various kinds of *Gouvernements Noten* (government notes) issued by the Zuid-Afrikaansche Republic (South African Republic).

Figure 1: An *Een Pond* (one pound) issued in Pretoria on 28th May 1900.
$(8\frac{1}{16} \times 4\frac{5}{16}$ in. $- 20.6 \times 11.7$ cm.$)$

Figure 2: A *Vijf Pond* (five pounds) issued in Pietersburg on 1st April 1901.
$(8 \times 4\frac{5}{16}$ in. $- 20.3 \times 11.7$ cm.$)$

Figure 3: An *Een Pond* (one pound) issued *Te Velde* (in the field) on 1st May 1902.
$(7\frac{15}{16} \times 4\frac{1}{4}$ in. $- 20 \times 0.8$ cm.$)$
(*From the Oosthuizen Collection*)

Plate 185
A photograph of Major-General Baden-Powell's personal scrapbook, containing his own personal design drawings for the Mafeking Siege notes and copies of the £1, 10s., 3s., 2s. and 1s. notes issued.
(*By courtesy of The Scout Association, Baden-Powell House, London*)

Plate 186
Examples of the *Oranje Vrij Staat Post Noot* (Orange Free State Post Note) 10s., £1 and 1s.

(*By courtesy of the War Museum of the Boer Republics, Bloemfontein*)

108 Boer War Memorabilia

187

188

Plate 187
A 'Good For' two shillings issued by the Paymaster of the Border Scouts in Upington dated 1st March 1902.
(*By courtesy of the National Cultural History and Open-Air Museum, Pretoria*)

Plate 188
1s., 2s., 5s. and 10s. Green Point Track Prisoner-of-War Camp 'Good Fors'.
(*By courtesy of the National Cultural History and Open-Air Museum, Pretoria*)

Plate 189
Canteen 'Good For' notes issued by the prisoner-of-war camp at Bellevue, Simonstown: 6d., 1s., 2s., 5s. and 10s. notes.
(*By courtesy of the National Cultural History and Open-Air Museum, Pretoria*)

Plate 190
10 cents, 50 cents and 1 rupee 'Good For' notes issued by the Camp Commandant of the prisoner-of-war camps at Ragama and Diyatalawa.
(*By courtesy of the National Cultural History and Open-Air Museum, Pretoria*)

Plate 191
'Good For' notes for 5 cents, 10 cents, 25 cents, 50 cents, 1 rupee and 5 rupees issued by the Ceylon Ice & Cold Storage Co. Ltd. for use in the company's store in the Ragama Camp, Colombo, Ceylon.
(*By courtesy of the National Cultural History and Open-Air Museum, Pretoria*)

191

192

Plate 192

Figures 1 and 2: Examples of coins marked 'Imitation Kruger Sovereign'. There are many imitations. Some were made to be used as tokens on board games.

Figure 3: A 1s. size silver coin issued with the messsage '*Groete van Paul Kruger*' (Greetings from Paul Kruger) with the head of President Kruger on the reverse.
(*From the Oosthuizen Collection*)

Plate 193
A 'Koffyfontein Besieged' five pounds note.
(*By courtesy of the National Cultural History and Open-Air Museum, Pretoria*)

CHAPTER 8

Gold and Silver Memorabilia and Jewellery

A substantial number of gold and silver coins were turned into items of jewellery. All kinds of brooches, pendants for neck-chains or bracelets and rings were made from these coins.

Pictures of Boer War generals were also popular items to have framed in gold or silver to become 'charms' on a bracelet or to be worn as a pendant on a neck-chain or to be used for cuff-links and so on.

Silver and gold watches and their chains are also popular collectors' items.

Manufacturers produced a huge variety of silver items, ranging from one-of-a-kind presentation caskets and statuettes of generals sitting on their horses to the smaller items like cigarette cases, vestas, money containers, picture frames, ashtrays, letter-openers and a great variety of spoons. Silver cutlery carrying a regimental coat-of-arms or the coats-of-arms of the South African Republics is also collected.

In addition, personal items belonging to those who participated in the Boer War, and used or wore the items during the campaign in South Africa, are sought after.

Most of the silver items carry hallmarks and these enable the collector to determine whether or not the items were manufactured during the Boer War period.

Plate 194
A tiny gold pocket knife made by I. F. Ebersohn from a South African Republic gold sovereign taken from the pocket of a fallen Boer.
(*By courtesy of the War Museum of the Boer Republics, Bloemfontein*)

Plate 195
A gold brooch made from a ZAR (South African Republic) *Veldpond* (field pound) with the engraving 'J. P. Anno 1900' surrounded by four guns.
(*By courtesy of the War Museum of the Boer Republics, Bloemfontein*)

Plate 196
Examples of gold jewellery made from ZAR (South African Republic) gold coins. Pendants, brooches and cuff-links.
(*From the Oosthuizen Collection*)

Gold and Silver Memorabilia and Jewellery   115

Plate 197
Examples of silver jewellery made from ZAR (South African Republic) silver coins. Pendants, brooches and cuff-links.
(*From the Oosthuizen Collection*)

Plate 198
Figure 1: A gold (9ct.) pendant with a photograph of President Kruger.
(1½ in. – 3.8 cm.)

Figure 2: A silver brooch with the Crown and Union Jack and the coats-of-arms of the Transvaal and the Orange Free State.
Marker's mark: Max Mink & Co. Sterling, Patent Durban. (1¾ in. – 4.5 cm.)
(*From the Oosthuizen Collection*)

Plate 199

Figure 1: A European silver chain with a ZAR (South African Republic) silver coin.

Figure 2: A silver pocket watch engraved 'Siege of Ladysmith 118 days 1899–1900 W. Burwood L.S. H.M.S. Powerful' on a Birmingham silver chain with a silver ZAR 2s.

Figure 3: A silver pocket watch. On the face the name 'Thomas Holmes'. On the back a crest and on the inside of the back flap the engraving: 'Boer War 1899–1902 Sergt T. Holmes Army Service Corps 1st Division'.

Figure 4: A Birmingham silver chain with a ZAR 2s. silver coin.
(*From the Oosthuizen Collection*)

Plate 200
A miscellaneous collection of silver brooches.
(*From the Oosthuizen Collection*)

Gold and Silver Memorabilia and Jewellery   117

Plate 201
A silver charm bracelet with 'charms' containing the portraits of the Generals Dundonald, Baden-Powell, Kelly-Kenny and Lord Roberts.
(*By permission of the Africana Museum, Johannesburg*)

Plate 202
A pair of silver cuff-links (1900) with the crest of the East Surrey Regiment.
(*By permission of the National Army Museum, London*)

Plate 203
Miscellaneous jewellery. Cuff-links and charm pendants, with pictures of generals were popular. Some have metal frames, some have silver or gold frames.
(*From the Oosthuizen Collection*)

204

Plate 204

Two silver forks and a silver spoon with the coats-of-arms of the Orange Free State and the South African Republic.
(*By courtesy of the War Museum of the Boer Republics, Bloemfontein*)

Plate 205

Figure 1: A silver butterknife with a figure of 'The Handy Man' on the handle. Birmingham silver 1899.

Figure 2: A silver spoon with the figure of 'Tommy Atkins'. On the back 'S. Africa 1900'. Birmingham silver 1899.

Figure 3: A silver spoon with the figure of 'A Gentleman in Kharki'. On the back 'S. Africa 1900'. Sheffield silver 1899.

Figure 4: A silver spoon with a kneeling soldier and two guns as the handle. Birmingham silver 1900.

Figure 5 and 7: European silver spoons with ZAR silver coins on the handles.

Figure 6: A silver spoon made from two ZAR 1s. silver coins.

Figure 8: (At the bottom) A silver spoon with a 'Lee-Metford' gun as a handle and engraved 'Souvenir of the Anglo-Boer War 1899–1901'. London silver 1900.
(*Figure 6 by courtesy of J. D. and C. C. Zackon; the others from the Oosthuizen Collection*)

Plate 206

Silver teaspoons with Boer War generals. Spoon No. 6 with the motto 'Now and forever' depicts the killing of a boar (Boer). All the spoons with the exception of No. 7 are of Chester silver 1899.

Spoon No. 7, of General White, is made from Birmingham silver 1899.
(*From the Oosthuizen Collection*)

Gold and Silver Memorabilia and Jewellery   119

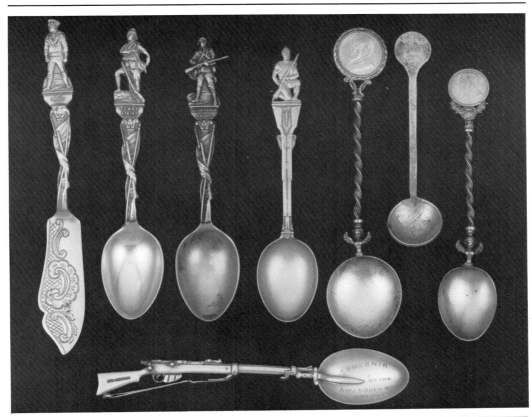
205

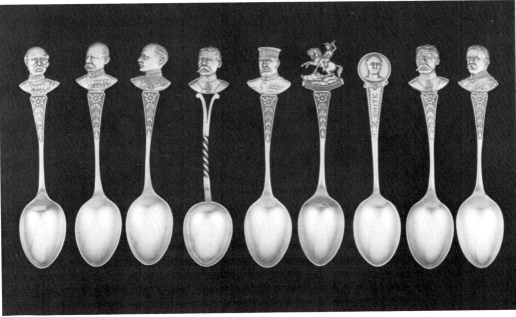
206

Plate 207
A silver fork and spoon and a knife with a part-silver handle.
Each of the items carries the following engraving:

'Lichtenburg
Rietfontein
Mafeking
7 Sep. 1899
23 Nov.
Modderriver
1 Dec. 1899 – 10 Feb. 1900
Schotsplaats
10 Feb. – 21 Feb.

Petrusburg
21 Feb. – 11 April
Brandfort
11 April – 16 June 1900'.
(*By courtesy of the War Museum of the Boer Republics, Bloemfontein*)

Plate 208
Silver items.
Top row
Figure 1: A silver money container with a crest engraved 'South Africa 1900–02'.
(3 in. – 7 cm.)

Gold and Silver Memorabilia and Jewellery   121

Figure 2: A silver picture frame with a picture of General French. Birmingham silver 1900. (2½ × 1⅝ in. – 6.3 × 4.2 cm.)

Figure 3: A small silver tray with a picture of Lord Kitchener in the centre. (2¾ in. – 7 cm.)

Middle row
Figure 4: A silver cigarette case with the engraving of 'A Gentleman in Kharki'. Chester silver 1899. (3 × 2½ in. – 7.6 × 6.3 cm.)

Figure 5: A silver vesta engraved 'W.C.C. Elm House to Pt. J. E. Edwards 71 C.I.V. on his return from South Africa Nov. 7th 1900'.
Birmingham silver 1900. (1⅞ × 1⅞ in. – 4.8 × 4.8 cm.)

Figure 6: A silver vesta with an enamelled coat-of-arms of the Transvaal. Birmingham silver 1904. (2⅛ × 1½ in. – 5.3 × 3.8 cm.)

Figure 7: A silver vesta with a picture of Lord Roberts and embossed 'General Bobs'. Marked: Solid Excel Silver Pat. Appd. for Reg. No. 331425. (2 × 1⅜ in. – 5 × 3.5 cm.)

Bottom row
Figure 8: A silver vesta with a figure of 'A Gentleman in Kharki'. Birmingham silver 1899. (2 × 1¾ in. – 5 × 4.5 cm.)

Figure 9: A round silver box with the figure of 'A Gentleman in Kharki'. Birmingham silver 1899. (1½ in. – 3.8 cm.)

Figure 10: A silver-plated vesta with the figure of 'A Gentleman in Kharki'. (2⅛ × 1¾ in. – 5.3 × 4.5 cm.)
(*Figure 9 by courtesy of J. D. and C. C. Zackon; others from the Oosthuizen Collection*)

Plate 209
Miscellaneous silver items.

Top left: Five copper serviette rings with silver tags bearing the names of battles: Tugela, Naudee's Kop, Spion Kop, Talana and Gun Hill.

Bottom left: A white metal figure of 'A Gentleman in Kharki'.
(5¼ in. – 13.3 cm.)

Centre: A silver letter-opener with a ZAR (South African Republic) 1 penny copper coin on top. (7½ in. – 19 cm.)

Top right: A glass jar with a silver top with the figure of 'A Gentleman in Kharki' Birmingham silver 1900.
(3½ in. high × 3¾ in. wide – 8.9 × 9.5 cm.)

Bottom right: A white metal ashtray with the figure of Lord Roberts embossed in the centre.
(3½ in. – 8.9 cm.)

(*From the Oosthuizen Collection*)

Plate 210
A silver box made from ZAR (South African Replubic) coins with the engraving 'D. P. Brink aan *M. T. Steyn Oorlog* 1899 *Vrede* 1902' (D. P. Brink to M. Y. Steyn war 1899 peace 1902).

(*By courtesy of the War Museum of the Boer Republics, Bloemfontein*)

Gold and Silver Memorabilia and Jewellery 123

Plate 211
A silver-plate commemorative carriage clock surrounded by a parcel-gilt plate embossed with a regimental coat-of-arms flanked by the inscription 'South Africa' and '1900–1901'. The inscription at the bottom reads 'Presented to Farrier R. Martin I.Y. in Recognition of Patriotic Service in the South African Campaign, Helensburgh June 1901'. Maker's mark: E & Co. Ld, London 1901 key. ($8\frac{7}{16}$ in. – 21.5 cm.)
(By courtesy of the Africana Museum, Johannesburg; photograph by courtesy of Sotheby's, Johannesburg)

Plate 212

One of the silver belts presented to the nursing sisters of the Assembly Military Hospital, Pietermaritzburg, Natal during the Boer War.

(By permission of the Africana Museum, Johannesburg)

Plate 213

Figure 1: A tin game: 'Oom Paul gets his teeth drawn' with a silver-backed mirror on the reverse side. ($2\frac{1}{2}$ in. – 6.3 cm.)

Figure 2: A silver 'A Gentleman in Kharki' place-card holder. ($2\frac{3}{4}$ in. – 7 cm.)

Figure 3: Silver cigarette-case with an enamelled picture of 'A Gentleman in Kharki'. ($3\frac{3}{8} \times 2\frac{1}{2}$ in. – 8.5 × 6.3 cm.)

Figure 4: Silver place-card holder — a gun with a silver ZAR (South African Republic) 1s. piece.

Figure 5: A silver spoon with Lord Roberts on the handle, marked 'South Africa 1900'. ($5\frac{1}{2}$ in. – 14 cm.)

Figure 6: Silver pocket watch with a picture of President Kruger and a ZAR (South African Republic) coat-of-arms in the seconds' dial. Inscribed 'A. le Roux — *Bombardier in die Artillerie, Kamp* Pretoria, Transvaal' (bomber in the Artillery, Camp Pretoria, Transvaal).

(All from the collection of Mr Kenneth Griffith, London)

Plate 214

A silver lion with a crown presented to the Transvaal Deputation by J. M. van Kempen & Zn., Voorschoten, Holland.
(6 in. – 15.2 cm.)

(By courtesy of the National Cultural History and Open-Air Museum, Pretoria)

Plate 215

A silver Swiss pocket watch with portraits of the Boer generals De la Rey, Botha, Joubert, De Wet and Cronje on its face.

(By courtesy of the War Museum of the Boer Republics, Bloemfontein)

Gold and Silver Memorabilia and Jewellery 125

214

215

CHAPTER 9

Tin and Pewter Memorabilia

Tin and pewter have been popular for centuries. The charm of pewter lies in its satiny-grey colour and its pleasing texture. Pewter is reported to have been known and used in ancient Egypt, ancient Japan and ancient China. Phoenicians traded in tin and lead with Britain. Many believe the Roman occupation of Britain most probably had much to do with the local tin and lead deposits. In Britain the tin comes from Cornish mines.

The best quality pewter ware is made entirely from tin. However, cheaper pewter ware is manufactured from tin alloyed with lead, antimony and/or copper. Ancient pewter usually contained a great amount of lead.

In the past, pewter jugs, mugs and tankards were in great demand. Pewter ware was also used in households for display.

The industrial revolution saw the use of tin in the manufacture of a vast range of mass-produced items such as tin containers.

A variety of tin and pewter items was produced in the United Kingdom and Europe to commemorate Boer War events. The range is very wide. Pewter mugs were manufactured, as well as many tin plates, ashtrays, tea canisters and tobacco tins.

Plate 216

Figure 1: (at the back) A tin plate with a picture of 'Field Marshall Lord Roberts V.C.' in the centre. On the rim pictures of 'Lord Kitchener, Maj-Gen. Pole Carew, Maj-Gen. Kelly-Kenny, Gen. Hector MacDonald'.
($11\frac{3}{4}$ in. – 29.9 cm.)
(*One of a series of plates with the pictures of generals*)

Figure 2: (at the back) A tin tea caddy in the form of a shell marked 'Facsimile of Shell — Memento of the Transvaal War 1899 – 1900'. Marked on the bottom 'Registered Design — Packed by the British & Benington's Tea Trading Asso'n Limited, 118 Southwark St., London John Wilson, Tin Printer. Shipley Sole Maker'.
($9\frac{1}{4}$ in. – 23.5 cm. high: $3\frac{3}{4}$ in. – 9.5 cm. wide)

Figure 3: (in front) A tin tea canister. On the lid a picture of 'Major-General Baden-Powell' and on the sides pictures of 'Lord Roberts, Gen. French, Gen. Sir Redvers Buller and Lord Kitchener'.
($6\frac{1}{4} \times 4 \times 4$ in. – 15.9 × 10.2 × 10.2 cm.)

128   Boer War Memorabilia

Figure 4: (in front) A modern tin now on sale in stores in London. On the lid a picture of 'Major-General Baden-Powell' and on the sides pictures of 'Lord Roberts, Lt. Gen. Lord Methuen, Lord Kitchener and Gen. Sir Redvers Buller'.

(Octagonal — $5\frac{1}{4} \times 5\frac{3}{4} \times 3\frac{3}{4}$ in. – $13.3 \times 14.6 \times 9.5$ cm.)

Figure 5: (in front) Another tin plate from the series. In the centre a picture of 'Lieut-General J. D. P. French' and on the rim pictures of 'Col. Kekewich, Gen. Sir C. F. Clery, Gen. Sir H. M. Leslie Rundee and Maj. Gen. Wauchope'.

($11\frac{3}{4}$ in. – 29.9 cm.)

(*All from the Oosthuizen Collection*)

216

Plate 217

Figure 1: An enamelled tin cup with a picture of King Edward inscribed '1902' and 'Peace with honour' and flanked by pictures of 'General de Wet', 'Pax', 'Lord Kitchener' and 'Britannia'. (3 in. – 7.6 cm.)

Figure 2: A tin plate with a picture of Queen Victoria in the centre surrounded with pictures of General French, Lord Roberts, General Buller, General White, Lord Kitchener and Lieutenant-Colonel Baden-Powell. On the ribbon between the pictures: Kimberley, Ladysmith, Bloemfontein, Mafeking.

($9\frac{1}{2}$ in. – 24.1 cm.)

(*From the collection of Mr Kenneth Griffith, London*)

Plate 218

Figure 1: An ashtray with a picture of 'Major-General French' flanked by two soldiers with the inscription: 'England expects every man to do his duty' and 'Soldiers of the Queen'.
(4 in. – 10.2 cm.)

Figure 2: A metal tray with a picture of General Baden-Powell flanked by flags, a lion and a laurel branch with the inscription 'Our B.P.'. (7 in. – 17.8 cm.)

Figure 3: A round tray with a picture of 'Lord Roberts' with the inscription 'Souvenir of South Africa 1899 – 1900'.
(3 in. – 7.6 cm.)

Figure 4: An ashtray with a picture of 'Lord Roberts V.C.' flanked by two soldiers with the inscription 'England expects every man to do his duty' and Soldiers of the Queen'.
(4 in. – 10.2 cm.)
(*Figure 2 from the collection of Mr Kenneth Griffith, London; others from the Oosthuizen Collection*)

Plate 219

Figure 1: A tin with a picture of a 'Handyman' on the lid. On the sides pictures of 'Cecil Rhodes' and 'The Proposed Railway — Route from Cairo to the Cape'; 'Rhodesian Horse' and 'Uitlander meeting on the Market Square, Johannesburg. Cape Town Highlanders, Natal Carbineers, Cape Mounted Rifles'; 'China' and 'Lord Charles Beresford'; 'Lord Kitchener of Khartoum'.
($6\frac{1}{2} \times 4 \times 4$ in. – 16.5 × 10.2 × 10.2 cm.)

Figure 2: A tin with 'Field Marshal Lord Roberts' on the lid. On the sides the following pictures: 'Lord Roberts entering Bloemfontein', 'Bringing up the guns', 'Lord Roberts entertainment of the Military Attaches at Pretoria' and 'The Outposts'. On the bottom: 'Keen, Robinson & Co. Ltd. Manufacturers of Keen's Mustard, London.'
($8 \times 7\frac{3}{4} \times 7\frac{3}{4}$ in. – 20.3 × 19.7 × 19.7 cm.)

Figure 3: A soap powder tin with the label marked 'Skirmisher Bright Flake' and a Boer War picture.
($1\frac{3}{4} \times 4 \times 7\frac{1}{4}$ in. – 4.5 × 10.2 × 18.4 cm.)

Figure 4: A tin with the following pictures on the sides: 'Col. Robert S. S. Baden-Powell Defender of Mafeking', 'Sir Redvers Buller', 'Lord Kitchener' and 'Lieut. Gen. Sir George White V.C. G.C.B. Ladysmith, Natal, S.A.'.
($4 \times 5\frac{1}{2} \times 8\frac{3}{4}$ in. – 10.2 × 14 × 22.2 cm.)
(*All from the collection of Mr Kenneth Griffith, London*)

Boer War Memorabilia

219

220

221

222

Plate 220
A tin tea caddy showing scenes of the career of Lord Roberts, with military awards and medals and decorations. The caddy carries the following pictures: 'Field Marshall Lord Roberts Commander in Chief'. 'The ovation to Roberts when leaving Afghanistan', 'Roberts saving the Colours', 'Roberts hoisting the British Flag on Mess House at Lucknow' and 'Surrender of Cronje'.
   ($6\frac{1}{8} \times 3\frac{15}{16} \times 4\frac{1}{16}$ in. – $15.5 \times 10 \times 10.3$ cm.)
(*By permission of the Africana Museum, Johannesburg*)

Plate 221
A tin tea canister with pictures of General De Wet, General Botha and General Delarey.
(*By courtesy of the National Cultural History and Open-Air Museum, Pretoria*)

Plate 222
Tin tea canisters issued in three sizes by 'Zonatura Tea, From the Sweet Scented Island Ceylon — Rich & Fragrant' with the coat-of-arms of the South African Republic.
(*By courtesy of the National Cultural History and Open-Air Museum, Pretoria*)

Tin and Pewter Memorabilia 131

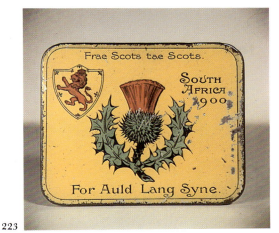

Plate 223

Plate 223
A tobacco tin sent to the Scottish Regiments in the Boer War, marked 'Frae Scots tae Scots — South Africa 1900 — For Auld Lang Syne'.

($3\frac{7}{8}$ in. – 9.9 cm.)
(*By courtesy of Rita & Ian Smythe, Britannia, London*)

Plate 225
A tobacco tin sent to the Devon Regiment, marked '*Semper Fidelis*', 'From the 3rd & 4th Battalions to the 1st & 2nd', 'Devon Regiment' and 'South Africa Xmas 1901'.

($3\frac{1}{8} \times 4\frac{1}{2} \times 1$ in. – $8 \times 11.5 \times 2.5$ cm.)
(*By permission of the Africana Museum, Johannesburg*)

Plate 224
Two chocolate tins. Queen Victoria sent a tin to each Soldier in South Africa. The tins carry an embossed picture of Queen Victoria with the inscription 'South Africa 1900' and in the writing of the Queen 'I wish you a happy New Year'. The tins were designed by Messrs J. S. Fry and Sons, Bristol, who sent 40,000 tins to South Africa. The rest of the tins were made and sent by Messrs Cadbury and Rowntree. (6 in. – 15.2 cm.)
(*From the Oosthuizen Collection*)

Plate 226
A tin plaque mounted on wood engraved with the figure of 'A Gentleman in Kharki'.
(*By permission of the National Army Museum, London*)

Plate 227
A cylindrical pewter mug inscribed 'Commemoration Cup Transvaal War 1899–1900'. Two crossed flags and 'Lord Roberts V.C. Commander in Chief'.
Base rim marked "59/5 Mess 15/21 Hussars 1911.
(*By courtesy of Sotheby's, Johannesburg*)

Plate 228
Figure 1: A German pewter mug with the following scenes: a picture of President Kruger marked 'President Kruger'; a picture of a monument marked '*Monte Paarde Kraal*'; the coat-of-arms of the ZAR (South African Republic), inscribed, '*Eendracht maakt magt*' (unity is strength); and the parliament building in Pretoria marked '*Reg. Geb. te Pretoria*'.
Maker's mark : L. Roehlin, Muenchen.
(4½ in. – 11.4 cm.)

Figure 2: A German pewter mug with impressed pictures of 'General Baron Herbert Kitchener' and 'Field Marshall Lord Roberts'.
Maker's mark : N.B.M. Gesetzlic Geschützt.
(4⅝ in. – 11.7 cm.)
(*Both from the Oosthuizen Collection*)

Tin and Pewter Memorabilia   133

Plate 229
A picture frame. Around the frame pictures of the Boer War soldiers and arms. (10½ in. – 26.7 cm.) In front two small brass figures of 'A Gentleman in Kharki' and 'The Handyman'. (3½ in. – 8.9 cm.)
(All from the collection of Mr Kenneth Griffith, London)

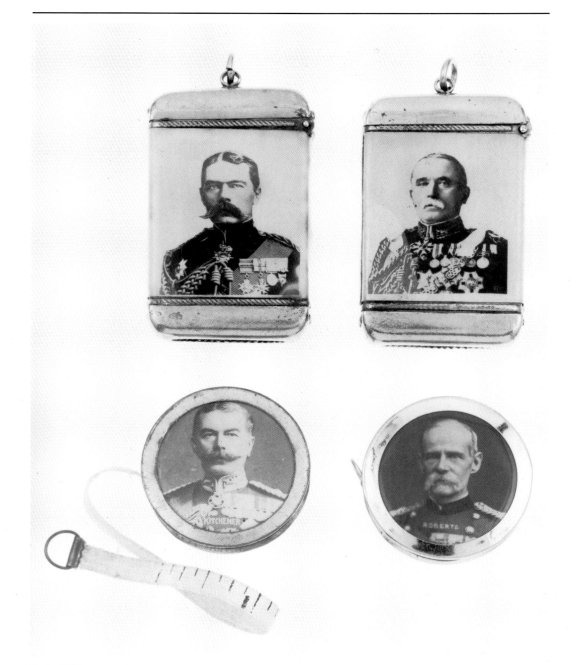

Plate 230

Top row: Two tin vestas from a series issued with generals. The first with a picture of Lord Kitchener and the second with a picture of General French. (2⅜ in. – 6 cm.)

Second Row: Two tin tape-measures from a series. The first with a picture of Lord Kitchener and the second with a picture of Lord Roberts. (1½ in. – 3.8 cm.)

(*From the Oosthuizen Collection*)

Tin and Pewter Memorabilia   135

Plate 231
Two small embossed metal picture frames. Both with pictures of Major-General Baden-Powell.
Top frame: With embossed words 'Mafeking' and '1900'.
$(1\frac{3}{4} \times 1\frac{1}{2}$ in. -4.5×3.8 cm.$)$
Bottom frame: Embossed in 'diamante' style.
$(2\frac{1}{2}$ in.:6.4 cm.$)$
(*Top frame from the Oosthuizen Collection; bottom frame by courtesy of Mr Kenneth Griffith, London*)

Plate 232

Figure 1: A pewter salt cellar with maps of the Transvaal and the Orange Free State and the words 'The Late Boer Republics'.
$(3\frac{5}{8}$ in. -9.2 cm.$)$
(*From the Oosthuizen Collection*)

Figure 2: A flat lead figure of a mounted soldier with the words 'Boer War' and '1899–1900'. $(3$ in. -7.6 cm.$)$
(*By courtesy of Mr Kenneth Griffith, London*)

CHAPTER 10

Ephemera

Commemorative letters, photographs, maps, newspapers and magazines, cigarette cards, posters, music, postcards, tickets, etchings, caricatures, illustrations, games, sermons, advertisements, announcements, official documents.

Stories and pictures of wars have always fascinated those not involved in them. During the Boer War, letters, memoirs, maps, photographs and news reports became the mode of communication with the people away from the war front.

When hostilities were over, much of the paperwork associated with the war, such as transport vouchers, maps, official announcements, personal documents of the soldiers and documents on supplies, hospitals and movements of troops, became collectibles.

The material produced on the home front, such as newspapers, magazines, sheet music, cigarette cards, caricatures and cartoons and books, also became highly prized by collectors.

Demand for information at home became so great that during the Boer War the first illustrated history of a war was published. The Boer War also produced a flood of coloured illustrations of commanding officers, the various troop units and the sieges and major battles.

ADDRESSES, COMMEMORATIVE LETTERS AND POSTERS

This is a very interesting field for collectors. Many of the 'thank-you' letters, commemorative letters and posters, and tributary addresses have magnificent artwork around their borders. Special mention should be made of all the addresses from Russian towns and villages to the Boer generals. Very imaginative work was also done by POWs in the addresses they prepared.

138 Boer War Memorabilia

Plate 233
An illuminated address (commemorative letter) from the St. Helena prisoners of war to Mrs A. S. Green (work done by Dirk Jansen and Erich Mayer).
(*By permission of the Africana Museum, Johannesburg*)

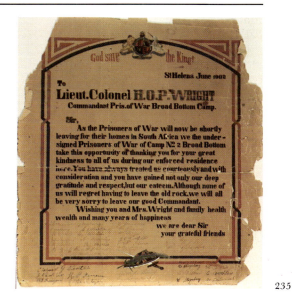

Plate 235
A 'thank-you' letter to Lieutenant Colonel H. O. P. Wright, Commandant of Broad Bottom Camp, St. Helena, signed by Boer prisoners of war.
(*By courtesy of the War Museum of the Boer Republics, Bloemfontein*)

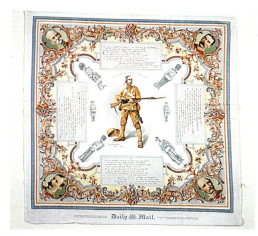

Plate 234
A commemorative poster for 'The Absentminded Beggar' with a colourful border containing pictures of Boer war generals.
$(39\tfrac{1}{2} \times 39\tfrac{1}{2}$ in. $- 1 \times 1$ m.$)$
(*By permission of the Africana Museum, Johannesburg*)

Plate 236
An elaborately decorated commemorative address from Germany to General De Wet, in a tooled leather cover.
(15 × 12 in. – 38.1 × 30.5 cm.)
(*By courtesy of the War Museum of the Boer Republics, Bloemfontein*)

PHOTOGRAPHS

By the time of the Boer War, cameras were in general use, and were carried by both officers and troops as well as by newsmen. There are as a result many thousands of photographs in the archives of museums and publishers and in the hands of private collectors. These photographs cover all the phases and aspects of the war.

Some collectors are solely interested in photographs, and will often take this specialization further, collecting only those which depict a particular aspect of the war. Those whose enthusiasm is of a more general nature, however, will usually have a number of photographs in their collections.

Plate 238
A photograph of one of the blockhouses built during the second phase of the Boer War.
(*By permission of the National Army Museum, London*)

Plate 237
A photograph of British soldiers crossing the Vaal River.
(*By permission of the National Army Museum, London*)

Plate 239
A photograph of Boer leaders: Commandant Van Deventer, General Smuts and Commandant Maritz.
(*By permission of the National War Museum, London*)

Plate 240
A photograph of the winding-up or the clearing of a Boer farm (burning a cape-cart).
(By permission of the National Army Museum, London)

Plate 241
A photograph of 'Boers leaving St. Helena for their homes in South Africa 26.6.02'.
(By permission of the National Army Museum, London)

Plate 242
A photograph of four mounted Boers with their rifles.
(By permission of the National Army Museum, London)

241

242

MAPS

There are collectors who are only interested in maps, including general maps of South Africa or the Transvaal or Orange Free State, and maps of towns and their surrounding areas. For specialists there are also maps of battle fields.

Plate 243
A 'Map of South Africa showing Frontiers, Rivers, Railways and Places mentioned in the Text' 1900.
(From the collection of Mr Kenneth Griffith, London)

Plate 244
A map of Pretoria and the surrounding area by H. C. Simpson.
$(14\frac{3}{16} \times 16\frac{1}{2}$ in. $- 36 \times 42$ cm.)
(By courtesy of the Africana Museum, Johannesburg)

Plate 245
A map of Kimberley and its environs, which appeared in the publication 'Black and White Budget' of 23rd December, 1899.
(From the Oosthuizen Collection)

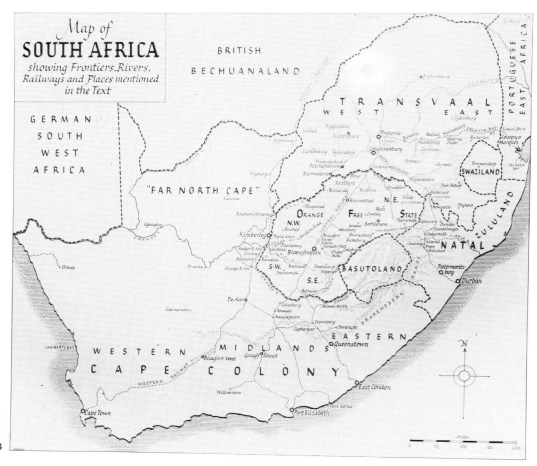

243

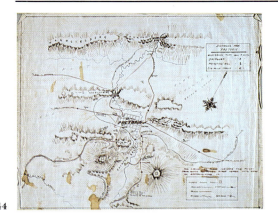

244

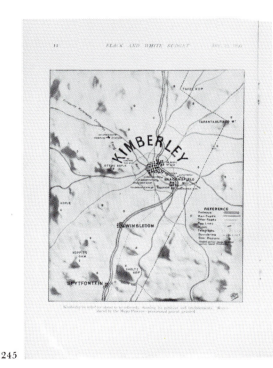

245

NEWSPAPERS AND MAGAZINES

Many of the newspapers and magazines published during the Boer War have become collectors' pieces. Many carried photographs or interesting illustrations of the events in the Boer War. The ones that have become most popular with collectors are:

(*a*) *The Graphic*, an illustrated weekly newspaper;
(*b*) *Ally Sloper's Half-Holiday*;
(*c*) *The Sphere*;
(*d*) *With the Flag to Pretoria*, issued fortnightly; all the issues were also bound into two volumes;
(*e*) *Under the Union Jack*, a weekly publication;
(*f*) *The Navy and Army Illustrated*;
(*g*) *Black & White*, periodical;
(*h*) *Vanity Fair*, their caricatures in colour are highly collectable;
(*i*) *Punch*, the cartoon etchings from this periodical are very popular;
(*j*) *Daily Express*, especially its 'Special Editions';
(*k*) *After Pretoria: The Guerilla War*, this periodical succeeded *With the Flag to Pretoria*, all the issues were also bound into a book.

The most collectable of the European magazines are:

(*a*) The French illustrated magazine *L'Assiette au Beurre*, which was also translated into German,
(*b*) *De Prins*, an illustrated magazine from Holland,
(*c*) *De Zuid-Afrikaansche Oorlog*, a Dutch publication by G. L. Kepper in twenty issues, which were also bound into a hard-cover book, excellent etchings of life in the Boer Republics.

Rare collector's pieces are the newspapers published in the prisoner-of-war camps. In Bermuda in the Camp at Burt's Island the POWs published a paper called *Die Burt's Trompet* (The Burt's Trumpet). In St. Helena at the Deadwood Camp they published *De Krygsgevange* (The Prisoner of War) and in Ceylon at the Diyatalawa Camp the newspaper *Diyatalawa Dum-Dum*. The British prisoners of war in the Boer prison camp in Pretoria published *The Pretoria Prisoner's Paper*. The British POWs in Pretoria also published *The Gram*.

During the Siege of Ladysmith the garrison published the *Ladysmith Bombshell*. This siege newspaper was edited by Earl Robert. The newspaper was published during the period of the Siege from 2nd November 1899 to 25th February 1900.

Plate 247
The Pretoria Prisoners' Paper. This paper was published in the main Boer prison camp in Pretoria by the British prisoners. This paper mentions 'Tommy Atkins' as a journalist.
(*By permission of the National Army Museum, London*)

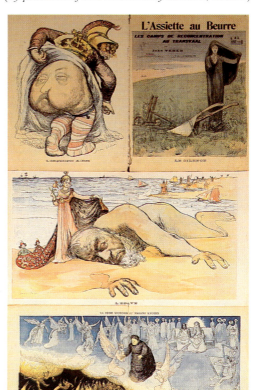

Plate 246
The cover page of the popular publication *Ally Sloper's Half-Holiday* dated Saturday 28th October 1899.
(*From the Oosthuizen Collection*)

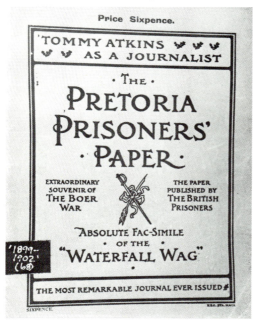

Plate 248
Some illustrations from the French publication *L'Assiette au Beurre*.
Top picture: The back and front picture of the magazine entitled *'L'Impudique Albion'* and *'Le Silence'*.
Middle picture: Entitled *'L'Epave'*.
Bottom picure: This sketch carries the title *'La Reine Victoria et Madame Kruger'* and *'Bonne Madame Kruger! Pourrez-vous jamais obtenir le pardon de cette reine cruelle!'*
(*From the Oosthuizen Collection*)

Ephemera 145

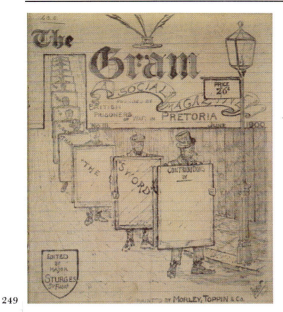

Plate 249
A photograph of *The Gram* of June 1900. This newspaper was founded by British POWs in Pretoria.
(*By permission of the National Army Museum, London*)

Plate 250
The *Ladysmith Bombshell*, the Ladysmith Siege newspaper edited by Earl Robert. This paper was published during the Siege of Ladysmith, 2nd November 1899 to 25th February 1900.
(*By permission of the Africana Museum, Johannesburg*)

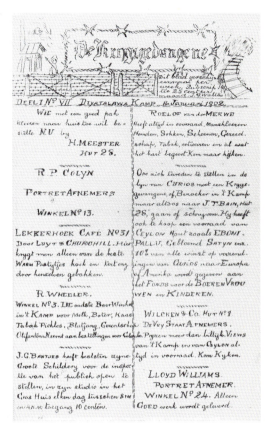

Plate 251
De Krygsgevangene (The Prisoner of War) the newspaper of the prisoners of war in the Diyatalawa Camp.
(*By courtesy of the National Cultural History and Open-Air Museum, Pretoria*)

Plate 252
De Strever (The Striver), a magazine published by the Church of Youth Organization in the Diyatalawa Camp in Ceylon.
(*By courtesy of the National Cultural History and Open-Air Museum, Pretoria*)

252

CIGARETTE AND OTHER CARDS

Towards the end of the nineteenth century, cigarette companies in the United States of America and Canada started to issue 'cigarette cards', or — as they were called at the time — 'tobacco inserts'. Today the collecting of cigarette cards — also called 'cartophily' — has become a popular hobby.

The following issues are of interest to the collectors of Boer War Memorabilia.

(a) 'Boer Leaders' issued by Taddy's (James Taddy & Co. of London) in 1901.
There were twenty cards in this series.

(b) 'V.C. Heroes — Boer War' issued by Taddy's in 1902.
There were sixty cards in this series.

(c) 'Victoria Cross Heroes' issued by Taddy's in 1904.
There were twenty-five cards in this series.

(d) In 1900–1901 W. D. & H. O. Wills of Bristol produced the 'Transvaal Series'.

(e) In 1895 Ogden of Liverpool started to issue series of cards. Many of these cards illustrate Boer War topics, more than 140 being known to be in this category. (The firm was later acquired by the American company Jas B. Duke.) They were the first to use real photographs on their cards.

(f) In 1895 W. D. & H. O. Wills of Bristol issued sets of cards entitled 'Soldiers and Sailors' and 'Ships'. Many of these cards are also being collected by Boer War enthusiasts.

In France the company Louit Frères & Co. of Bordeaux, makers of chocolates and importers of tea, issued a series of cards covering the 'Guerre du Transvaal'.

The same title was given to a series of cards issued by the Belgian store L. Gerome-Haniq of Ixelles-Bruxelles.

Plate 253
A photograph of twenty 'Ogden's' cigarette cards relating to the Boer War. More than 140 Boer War-related cards were issued by Ogden's.

Row 1: General Erasmus, Lieutenant-General Clery, General Botha, President Steyn, Colonel Baden-Powell.
Row 2: Ex-President Kruger, H.M. Queen Victoria, Lord Roberts, H.R.H.

Prince of Wales, Brigadier-General Brabant.

Row 3: 'Handyman', Lord Kitchener, Hon. J. Chamberlain, General White, Sir A. Milner.

Row 4: General Buller, Lieutenant-General Gatacre, Lieutenant-General French, Lord Methuen, General Cronje.

(*From the Oosthuizen Collection*)

254

Plate 254
Cigarette Cards: Eight cards from the Taddy's & Co. series on Boer leaders, with pictures of General Oliver, General Schiel, General Snyman, Commandant H. Pretorius, General Hans Erasmus, Commandant Kruitzinger, General Hendrik Schoeman and General Jan Kock.
In addition a card from the Taddy's & Co. series of V. C. Heroes — Boer War. This picture is of the Late Lieutenant F. Roberts V.C.

Chocolate and tea cards: Eight cards from the series issued by Louis Frères & Co., Bordeaux, covering the '*Guerre du Transvaal*' with pictures of:
'*Mort de Villebois-Mareuil à Boshop, 5 Avril 1900*'.

'*Bombardement de Ladysmith, 30 Octobre 1899*'.
'*Passage de la Tugela à Colenso 14 Decembre 1899*'.
'*L'artillerie anglaise à Rietfontein, 25 Octobre 1899*'.
'*Reddition d'un escadron anglais à Wryheid 20 Mai 1900*'.
'*Combat de Maggersfontein 12 Decembre 1899*'.
'*Prise de Colesberg par les Boërs, 3 Novembre 1899*'.
'*Les Grenadiers Anglais à Heilbron 29 Mai 1900*'.
(*From the Oosthuizen Collection*)

POSTERS
Posters cover a wide field from newspaper posters to theatre posters. Posters were issued to advertize merchandise or to publicise certain issues.

Plate 255
A large colourful picture-poster issued with a calendar in 1901 by Robert H. Bunner, Ironmonger, Montgomery, called 'Briton or Boer'.
The centre picture is of a mounted figure of 'Field Marshal Lord Roberts of Kandahar V.C. K.P. & C.,.
On the left side pictures of Colonel Plumer — Mafeking Relief Column, Major-General Hector A. MacDonald, Major-General Sir W. Gatacre, Major-General Lord Dundonald, surrender of Cronje to Lord Roberts.
On the right side pictures of General Joubert, President Kruger, President Steyn, General Cronje, and Relief of Ladysmith.
At the bottom, pictures of Major-General French, Colonel R. S. Baden-Powell, Sir George White V.C., Sir Redvers Buller V.C., Lord Kitchener, and Major-General Kelly-Kenny.
(*From the collection of Mr Kenneth Griffith, London*)

Plate 256
A popular poster entitled 'Like Father Like Son' with oval pictures of 'Field Marshal Lord Roberts V.C.,G.C.B.,G.C.S.I.,& C' and 'The Late Lieut. The Hon. F. H. S. Roberts V.C.' separated by a Victoria Cross, and below them a scene from 'The Battle of Colenso Decr. 15th 1899'.
(20 × 30 in. – 50.8 × 76.2 cm.)
(*From the Oosthuizen Collection*)

150 Boer War Memorabilia

Plate 257
Two posters depicting 'The British Leaders' in the 'Transvaal War 1899–1900'.

Poster 1: 'Field Marshall Right Hon. Lord Roberts V.C. G.C.B.' surrounded by Major-General H. J. T. Hidyard, Lieutenant-General T. Kelly-Kenny, Major-General J. D. P. French, Lieutenant-General Sir C. F. Clery, General Hector MacDonald, Lieutenant-General Sir Chas Warren, Lord Kitchener of Khartoum and Colonel R. G. Kekewich.

Poster 2: 'General Sir Redvers Buller' surrounded by Major-General Sir Archibald Hunter, Colonel Plumer, Lieutenant-General Lord Methuen, Major-General Sir W. F. Gatacre, Lieutenant-General Sir F. Forestier Walker, Colonel R. S. Baden-Powell, The Late General Sir W. P. Symons and Lieutenant-General Sir George White.
(*From the Oosthuizen Collection*)

Plate 258
A poster issued by the 'Stop the War' Committee at Clock House, Arundel St., London W.C. This poster was issued in many different sizes.
(*From the collection of Mr Kenneth Griffith, London*)

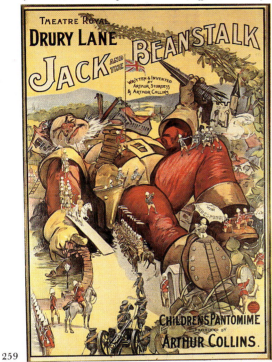

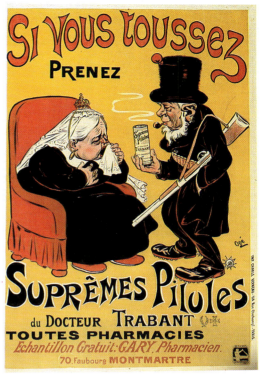

Plate 259
A Theatre Royal Drury Lane poster for the production *Jack and the Beanstalk* (with President Kruger as Jack), a childrens' pantomime produced by Arthur Collins and written and invented by Arthur Sturgess and Arthur Collins.
(21 × 31 in. – 53.3 × 78.7 cm.)
There was also another play produced by Arthur Collins at the Drury Lane Theatre called *The Best of Friends* for which many posters were issued with Boer War themes.
(*From the collection of Mr Kenneth Griffith, London*)

Plate 260
A French poster with Queen Victoria and President Kruger. '*Si vous toussez prenez Supreme Pilules*'.
(*By permission of the Africana Museum, Johannesburg*)

Plate 261

Figure 1: A *Liverpool Express* newspaper poster. The poster carries a picture of South Africa with a picture of Queen Victoria on top with the words 'United S. Africa'. Imposed on the map is a picture of Lord Roberts, and flanking it are pictures of General Baden-Powell and the Hon. J. Chamberlain. Below it are the words 'All red now Joey'.

Figure 2: A *Liverpool Express* newspaper poster. The poster carries a picture of the Imperial Lion standing on top of President Kruger in front of the Parliament Building in Pretoria, with the wording, 'Down, Kruger, down!!!' and 'PRETORIA!!!'.
(Both posters: 22 × 32 in. – 55.9 × 81.3 cm.)
(*From the Oosthuizen Collection*)

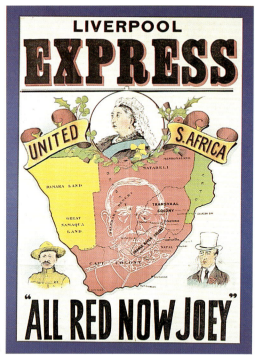

261

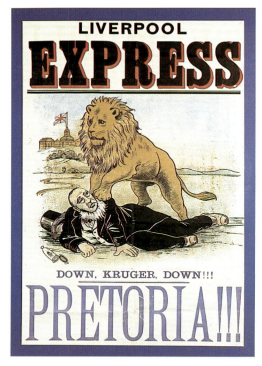

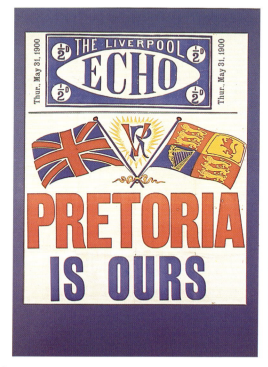

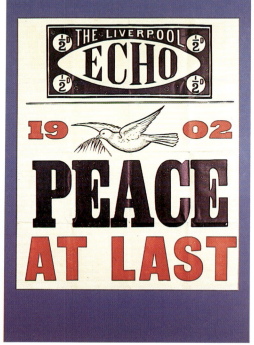

262

Plate 262

Figure 1: A poster of *The Liverpool Echo* dated Thursday 31st May 1900. The poster has a picture of two crossed flags, the letters V.R. and the words 'Pretoria is ours'.

Figure 2: A poster of *The Liverpool Echo* and the words '1902 PEACE at last'.
(Both posters: 22 × 32 in. – 55.9 × 81.3 cm.)
(*From the Oosthuizen Collection*)

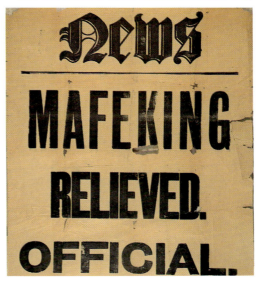

Plate 263

A small newspaper poster reading 'The Bloemfontein Post — June 1st, 1902 — Special – PEACE — Officially Declared — Details — Later'.
(6 × 4 in. – 15.2 × 10.1 cm.)
(*By courtesy of the War Museum of the Boer Republics, Bloemfontein*)

Plate 264

A newspaper poster reading:
'News. MAFEKING RELIEVED OFFICIAL'.
(*By courtesy of The Scout Association, Baden-Powell House, London*)

MUSIC

Writers and composers were inspired by the events of the Boer War. A great number of pieces were composed to honour events and personalities. In addition, new words were written for existing compositions to commemorate events.

Apart from all the music published in England and the rest of the Empire, a substantial number of pro-Boer compositions were published. The Kruger House Collection in Pretoria has recorded 128 items. The following countries are represented in this collection of published music:

- 1% Portugal
- 1% Italy
- 2% England & America
- 4% Russia
- 17% Germany
- 28% France
- 47% The Netherlands (including Belgium and compositions from the Cape and Transvaal published in the Netherlands)

In the prisoner-of-war camps many pieces were composed and recorded. Not all of these were published, however, and they have therefore become a scarce commodity.

In both England and Europe music covers were designed to promote the sales of the sheet music. Some of them are very colourful, and often have no obvious connection with the words or music inside. Those covers which feature Boer War decorations have become collectors' pieces, although the music they contain is of no interest.

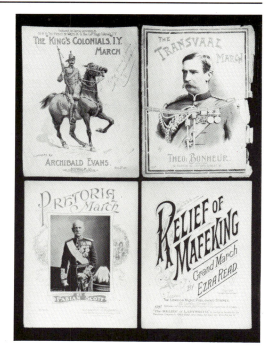

Plate 265
'The Peace Music Album' has an attractive and colourful cover. The album was issued 'In commemoration of the Settlement of Peace in South Africa'
Published by John G. Murdoch & Co. Ltd., London. ($12 \times 9\frac{5}{8}$ in. – 30.5×24.5 cm.)
(*From the Oosthuizen Collection*)

Plate 266
Examples of the music published during the Boer War.
1. 'The King's Colonials, I.Y. March' composed by Archibald Evans and published by Boosey & Co.
2. 'The Transvaal March' by Theo Bonheur, published by W. Paxton.
3. 'Pretoria March' by Fabian Scott, published by W. H. Broome.
4. 'Relief of Mafeking Grand March' by Ezra Read, published by The London Music Publishing Stores.

(*From the Oosthuizen Collection*)

Plate 267
The 'Regimental March of the 2nd County of London Imperial Yeomanry' composed by Geo. W. Byng and published by L. R. Lafleur & Son, London.
(*By permission of the Westminster Dragoons Museum Trust, London*)

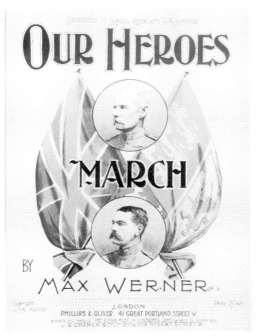

Plate 268
'Our Heroes March' by Max Werner, dedicated to Lords Roberts and Kitchener. Published by Phillips & Oliver, London.
(*By permission of the National Army Museum, London*)

Plate 269
'Baden-Powell March' by Aicrette, dedicated (by special permission) to General Baden-Powell. Published by J. B. Cramer & Co., London.
(*By permission of the National Army Museum, London*)

Plate 270
'Bravo! Dublin Fusiliers! or, Ireland's Reply' written and composed by G. D. Wheeler and published by Francis, Day & Hunter, London.
(*By permission of the National Army Museum, London*)

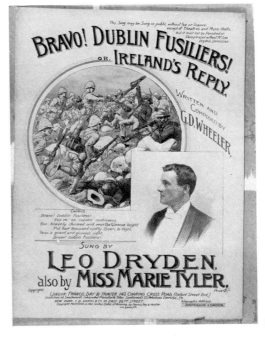

156 Boer War Memorabilia

Plate 271
'Our Boys' Waltz composed by Agnes Ella and published by B. J. Ewing & Co., Queenstown, C.C.
(*By courtesy of the National Cultural History and Open-Air Museum, Pretoria*)

Plate 272
'*Holland en Transvaal*' for Voice and Piano composed by Emil van den Eijnde, published by G. Alsbach, Amsterdam.
(*By courtesy of the National Cultural History and Open-Air Museum, Pretoria*)

Plate 273
'*Präsident Krüger Marsch*' by the Hungarian Composer Guido Pöcher.
(*By courtesy of the National Cultural History and Open-Air Museum, Pretoria*)

Ephemera 157

274

275

276

Plate 274
'*Trijdzang der Boeren*' composed by T. Pijper in Hardewijk, Holland, and published by De Holl. Stoomdr. & Uitgevers Maatsch., Amsterdam.
(*By courtesy of the National Cultural History and Open-Air Museum, Pretoria*)

Plate 275
'*Vaarwel!*' (Farewell), a song in memory of the War against the Transvaal and Free State 1899–1900, by J. H. L. Schumann, a Boer POW on St. Helena who composed many songs. Published by Egeling's Bookstore, Amsterdam.
(*By courtesy of the National Cultural History and Open-Air Museum, Pretoria*)

Plate 276
'*Vereenigd-Afrika*' (United Africa), song composed by Arnold Spoel, published by G. H. van Eck in The Hague.
(*By courtesy of the National Cultural History and Open-Air Museum, Pretoria*)

Plate 277
'*Engelsche Hazenmarsch opgedragen aan de Transvaalsche Boeren*' (The Hares' March, dedicated to the Transvaal Boers).
(*By courtesy of the National Cultural History and Open-Air Museum, Pretoria*)

277

278

Plate 278

'*Drei Schüsse Burenballade*' (Three Shots Boer Ballad) composed by Bernard Zweers, published by Van Holkema & Warendorf, Amsterdam.

(*By courtesy of the National Cultural History and Open-Air Museum, Pretoria*)

Plate 279

'*Generaal Joubert Marsch*' composed by Henri Lucas, published by Maison Blok, The Hague.

(*By courtesy of the National Cultural History and Open-Air Museum, Pretoria*)

279

POSTCARDS

This is another field with an extensive range of items, and one in which many collectors specialize. Postcards were commonly used at the turn of the century for writing short notes. Postcard greeting cards were also in general use — for example, for Christmas greetings.

In the Netherlands many thousands of postcards with Boer War and South African themes were sold to raise money for Boer War causes. In Europe many postcards with pro-Boer cartoons or caricatures were issued. In England many publishers issued cards to honour or commemorate the deeds of Empire soldiers or of specific regiments.

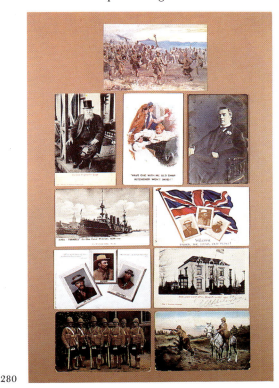

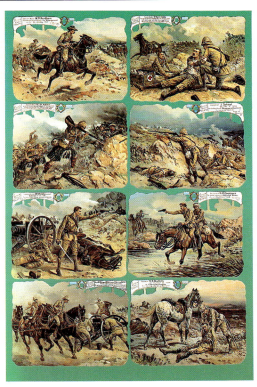

Plate 280
A sample of Boer War related postcards.
1. 'Meeting of the Battalions South Africa 1900'.
2. 'The Late Ex-President Kruger'.
3. 'Have one with me old chap. Kitchener won't mind'.
4. 'Rt. Hon. J. Chamberlain.'
5. 'H.M.S. *Terrible* (1st Class Cruiser (Protected) 14,200 tons').
6. 'De Wet, Botha, Delarey. Welcome under the dear old Flag!'
7. 'De Wet, Botha, Delarey. I had rather have such men my friends, than enemies. Let us swear an eternal friendship'.
8. 'Villa *Casa Cara* (Pres. Kruger's *verblijf* 1901)'. (President Kruger's home 1901)
(*From the Oosthuizen Collection*)

Plate 281
Very colourful glossy, embossed (raised) cut-outs from the Victoria Cross Gallery Series of Boer War V.C.

Row 1: 'Farrier-Major W. P. Hardham for conspicuous bravery near Naanpoort — 28 January 1901'.
'Surgeon-Captain A. Martin-Leake, during the action at Vlakfontein 8 February 1902 attended several wounded under heavy fire from 40 Boers at 100 yards until wounded 3 times'.
Row 2: 'Sargeant-Major William Robertson at the Battle of Elandslaagte 21 October, 1899 led each successive rush and captured enemy's position, being dangerously wounded in two places'.
'Corporal J. Schaul on Dec. 11 1899 at the Battle of Magersfontein for several specific acts of Bravery'.
*Row*3: Lieutenant the Hon. F. H. S. Roberts (deceased) Colenso 15 Dec. 1899 for con-

spicuous bravery, wounded in 3 places'.
'Lieutenant H. Z. C. Cockburn for great bravery on Komati River 7 November 1900'.
Row 4: 'Major Hornsby, Sergeant Parker*, Gunner Lodge**, Driver Glasock*. Action at Kornspruit 31 March 1900. This battery was treated as one of collective distinction * elected by non-commissioned officers ** elected by gunners and drivers'.
'Captain C. E. Mullins on October 21 1899 at Elandslaagte for saving life of a Trooper'.
(*From the collection of Mr Kenneth Griffith, London*)

282

283

284

Plate 282
Top: An envelope containing six postcards of 'Our Brave Defenders' issued by C. W. Faulkner & Co., London. Apart from the coat-of-arms and an appropriate phrase, the cards carry pictures of a Gunner, Royal Canadian Artillery, New South Wales Lancer, Trooper 1st Life Guards, Trooper 17th Lancers, Seaman Royal Navy, Private Royal Marine Light Infantry, Private Grenadier Guards and Trooper Royal Horse Guards.

Bottom: Cut-out pictures of Major-General Baden-Powell, Field Marshal Lord Roberts V.C., General Sir Redvers Buller V.C., Major-General French, General Sir George White V.C. and General Lord Kitchener.
(*The cards from the Oosthuizen Collection and the cut-outs from the collection of Mr Kenneth Griffith, London*)

Plate 283
An embroidered postcard with a crest and the wording '23rd Ba. The London Reg.' and 'South Africa 1900–02'.
(*By permission of the National Army Museum, London*)

Plate 284
A Belgian pro-Boer postcard with the inscription '*Wegvoering van gevangen Engelschen*' (Transport of captured English).
(*By permission of the National Army Museum, London*)

285

Plate 285
A Belgian pro-Boer postcard with the title '*Verovering van een gepantserden trein*' (Capture of an armoured train).
(*By permission of the National Army Museum, London*)

Plate 286
Dutch Boer War Postcards.
1. *Groet uit* (Greetings from) Kimberley.
2. *Groet uit* Elandslaagte.
3. *Groet uit* Ladysmith.
4. *Groet uit* Pietermaritzburg.
5. *Groet uit* Pretoria.
6. *Groet uit* Elandslaagte.
7. *Groet uit* Langs-Nek.
8. *Groet uit* Magersfontein.
9. *Groet uit* Mafeking.
(*From the Oosthuizen Collection*)

Plate 287
Boer War Christmas card with plants picked from the battlefields in Natal.
(*By courtesy of the National Cultural History and Open-Air Museum, Pretoria*)

Plate 288
Boer War Christmas card with dried plants picked from the battlefields in Natal.
(*By courtesy of the National Cultural History and Open-Air Museum, Pretoria*)

TICKETS, PASSES AND PERMITS

Tickets, passes and permits were issued in their thousands. Tickets to travel by rail and permits to perform certain duties, to enter camps, or to visit restricted areas, etc., were issued by both sides.

E 1205 IMPERIAL MILITARY RAILWAYS. T. 212.
73 Passengers' Ticket Single Journey.
Argus Co.—601. NOT TRANSFERABLE.
No. of Passengers (in words). Class (in words). Station from Amount.
PAARDEKOP
I.M.R.
Date Issued by

No. A 520 IMPERIAL MILITARY RAILWAYS. T. 238.
60 Passengers' Ticket Single Journey.
Argus Co.—597. NOT TRANSFERABLE.
No. of Passengers (in words). Class (in words). Station from Amount.
C.
Date Issued by

289

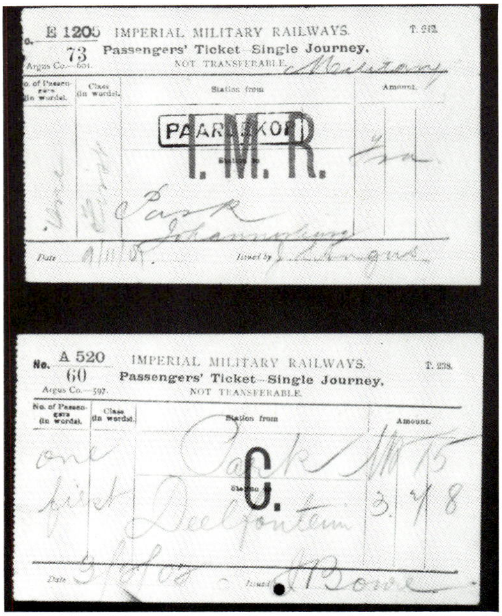

Plate 289

An example of Wartime rail tickets issued by the 'Imperial Military Railways'.

Figure 1: A ticket from Paardekop to Park Station (Johannesburg) dated 9th November 1901, stamped I.M.R. and marked 'Military'.

Figure 2: A ticket covering a journey from Park Station (Johannesburg) to Deelfontein dated 3rd February 1902, stamped 'C'.

(From the Oosthuizen Collection)

ETCHINGS, LITHOGRAPHS, CARICATURES AND ILLUSTRATIONS.

Most publications in the Empire and Europe at the turn of the century still used many coloured illustrations in addition to photographs. Cartoons and caricatures were also popular with the public.

Many of the recognized Boer War period artists used the medium of lithographs and etchings for their works.

290

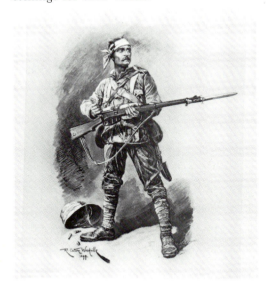

Plate 290

A lithographic reproduction of the drawing of 'The Absent-Minded Beggar' ('A Gentleman in Kharki') by the well-known artist R. Caton Woodville.

(By permission of the City of Bristol Museum and Art Gallery, Bristol)

291

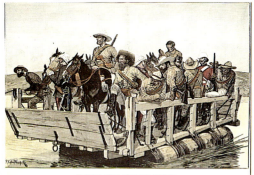

Plate 291

A coloured lithograph by R. Caton Woodville entitled 'The War in the Transvaal. Volunteers Crossing the Val River'.

(21 × 16½ in. – 53.3 × 41.9 cm.)

(From the Oosthuizen Collection)

Ephemera

Plate 292
An etching of 'Lord Roberts' by M. H. Long, 1901.
(*By permission of the National Army Museum, London*)

Plate 293
A caricature from *The Pretoria Prisoners Paper* issued by the British prisoners of war. '*Note.* The one pen in the possession of the Editorial Staff having given out, our artist wishes to apologise for the quality of these drawings — Ed.'.
(*By permission of the National Army Museum, London*)

Plate 294
Caricatures and cartoons which appeared in *Black and White Budget* magazines during the Boer War.
Top left: The map of Africa as the face of President Kruger, with all the British Possessions covered with Union Jack flags, and the title 'The New Map'.
Top right: A picture which could be turned upside-down, with the title: 'Two views of the War', 'Oom Paul before...and after'.
Bottom left: President Kruger looking at an empty lion's cage inscribed with the name Cecil Rhodes. The title reads: 'To be sold: The owner having no further use for it'.
Bottom right: Some Australian cartoons of the war.
(*From the Oosthuizen Collection*)

Plate 295
An etching entitled 'South African War' by F. J. Waugh.
(British troops leaving a farmyard.)
(*By permission of the National Army Museum, London*)

Plate 296
An etching entitled 'Retreat from Sanna's Post' by C. M. Sheldon, 1900.
(*By permission of the National Army Museum, London*)

295

296

Ephemera

Plate 297
Six Boer War caricatures and cartoons from the publication *Punch, or the London Charivari*.
(*From the Oosthuizen Collection*)

Plate 298
A German caricature of Joseph Chamberlain and Queen Victoria called 'The English Global Empire or Bloody Cartography'.
(*From the collection of Mr Kenneth Griffith, London*)

GAMES

Many kinds of games were produced during the period of the Boer War. Board games very popular, pro-British games being made in England and pro-Boer ones in Europe.

Many sets of playing cards with Boer War themes were produced. Trick games and games of skill were also manufactured.

The tokens for some of the board games — miniature soldier figures or replicas of coins — are also being collected, separately from the games.

Plate 299
A cardboard box with a glass-top skill game called 'Get the last nail in Old Kruger's Coffin'.
Pat. No. 25654.
$(4\frac{3}{4} \times 2\frac{1}{4} \times 1$ in. $- 12 \times 5.7 \times 2.5$ cm.$)$
(*From the Oosthuizen Collection*)

Boer War Memorabilia

Plate 300
A Dutch board game called '*Boer en Rooinekspel*' (Boer and Red-neck Game) manufactured by Gebr. Koster in Amsterdam.
($33\frac{1}{4} \times 23\frac{1}{2}$ in. – 85.7 × 59.7 cm.)
(*From the Oosthuizen Collection*)

Plate 301
A German 'Boer War' set of playing cards, produced by C. L. Wüst, Frankfurt.
(*By permission of the Africana Museum, Johannesburg*)

Plate 302
A set of playing cards which belonged to a Mr Herman Hendrik Smorenburg, who was a prisoner of war in the Ragama Camp in Ceylon.
(*By permission of the Africana Museum, Johannesburg*)

Plate 303
'The Great War Game'. A dice game with Boer and Briton lead tokens.
(*From the collection of Mr Kenneth Griffith, London*)

Plate 304
A Dutch board game called '*Dubbel Belegeringspel*' (Double Siege Game). Played with pegs.
(*By permission of the Africana Museum, Johannesburg*)

Plate 305
Four rows of 'cut-outs' for children, produced in Germany.
'Transvaal — Buren — Infantrie No. 9879'.
($16\frac{1}{2} \times 13\frac{1}{2}$ in. – 42 × 34 cm.)
(*By permission of the Africana Museum, Johannesburg*)

Ephemera

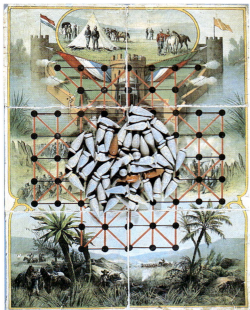

304

305

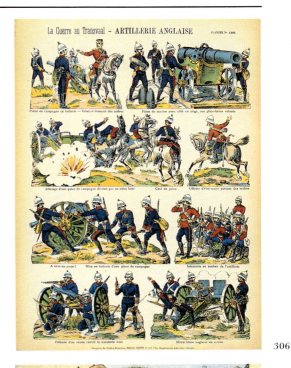

306

307

Plate 306
One of a series of children's 'cut-outs' with eight figures in colour, produced in France and marked 'La Guerre au Transvaal Artillerie Anglaise Planche No. 1101'.
(16 × 11½ in. – 40.5 × 28.5 cm.)
(*By permission of the Africana Museum, Johannesburg*)

Plate 307
A board game called 'How to reach Pretoria. The Great Transvaal War Puzzle'.
(*By permission of the Africana Museum, Johannesburg*)

Plate 308

A dice game called 'Boer or Briton — A new South African War Game'.

(*By permission of the National Army Museum, Johannesburg*)

Plate 309

A Dutch board game called 'Transvaal *Spel*' (Transvaal Game).

(*By courtesy of the War Museum of the Boer Republics, Bloemfontein*)

Plate 310

A board game entitled 'Boers vs. British or the War in South Africa'.
Marked Copyright 1902 by W. S. Hearst.
(*By courtesy of the War Museum of the Boer Republics, Bloemfontein*)

Plate 311

A Dutch postcard-size game entitled: '*Mik op Dum, Dum — Schietspel — Slag by Modderrivier*' (Aim at Dum-Dum — Shooting game — Battle of Modder River) with pictures of General Joubert and President Steyn, and in the centre a picture of President Paul Kruger holding the Hon. J. Chamberlain.
Published by Martin van Dam, Amsterdam.
(*By courtesy of the War Museum of the Boer Republics, Bloemfontein*)

BIBLES, PRAYERS AND SERMONS

Many sermons and/or special prayers delivered at services or at special occasions were published for general distribution. Some of the prayers and sermons were published in the form of booklets.

The United Home Churches in England published a 'New Testament' for general distribution to all the British soldiers in South Africa. These small Bibles have become a prized collectors' item.

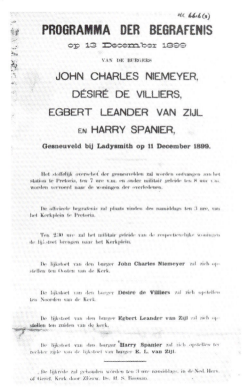

312

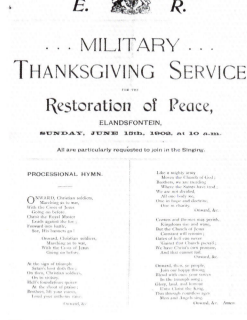

313

Plate 313
A copy of the programme of the 'Military Thanksgiving Service for the Restoration of Peace, Elandsfontein, Sunday June 15th 1902'.
(By courtesy of the National Cultural History and Open-Air Museum, Pretoria)

314

Plate 312
'*Programma der Begrafenis*' (Funeral Programme). A programme for the burial in Pretoria of Boer soldiers who died at Ladysmith on 11th December 1899.
A military march through Pretoria and a church service.
(By courtesy of the National Cultural History and Open-Air Museum, Pretoria)
See Plate No. 317 for details of the booklet *Brief Memoir of Col-Sergt. Macmillan: A Christian Colour-Sergeant*.

Plate 314
The New Testament distributed to the troops in South Africa.
On the cover: 'Soldier's New Testament' and 'South Africa 1900'.
On the inside page:

'Printed specially for Soldiers
Presented to:
belonging to the British Home and Colonial Forces engaged in South Africa, 1900, by the United Home Churches, with their greetings and prayers for personal blessings'.
$(4\frac{1}{2} \times 2\frac{7}{8}$ in. -11.5×7.3 cm.$)$
(From the Oosthuizen Collection)

ADVERTISEMENTS

The collection of advertisements has also become a field for specialists.

During the period of the Boer War many advertisers used Boer War themes to sell their products. Many of the advertisements referred only to products in use in South Africa or by the troops. Other advertisers used caricatures or famous Boer War symbols or figures to draw attention to their advertisement, although the product may have had nothing to do with the Boer War.

The greatest number of advertisements appeared in the newspapers and the magazines of the period. Some very attractive poster advertisements were also issued.

Top left: 'Stand by the old remedy — Beecham's Pills will right the constitutional wrongs' with a picture of a soldier.

Top right: 'Pioneer Tobacco' with a picture of President Kruger and John Bull facing one another.

Bottom left: 'Bovril at the Front and in the Front'. 'Bovril for Field Hospital use', etc., etc.

The above three appeared in the *Black and White Budget* magazine.

Bottom right: 'Kinnears Handicap Cigarettes'. The advertisement states that the packages of cigarettes contain 'an Exquisite Reproduction of Mr Caton Woodville's Great Picture Illustrating Rudyard Kipling's War Poem "An Absent-minded Beggar"'.
The above appeared in '*With the Flag to Pretoria*'
(All from the Oosthuizen Collection)

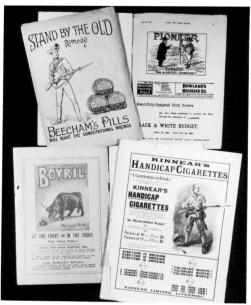

Plate 315
Advertisements in the publications *Black and White Budget* and *With the Flag to Pretoria*.

Plate 316
One of the most famous advertisements of the Boer War period.

Ephemera   171

A monkey handing President Kruger a box of 'Monkey Brand Cleanser and Polisher' with a picture of Joseph Chamberlain on the wall.
As published in *Ally Sloper's Half-Holiday* magazine on 28th October 1899.
(From the Oosthuizen Collection)

LETTERS AND SIGNATURES.

This is another highly specialized field. Letters and signatures of famous personalities or famous generals are always in demand and the prices for these items keep on rising.

Letters or signatures of the best-known or best-loved generals like Lord Roberts and Baden-Powell will always be in demand, as will letters from the field from celebrities such as Winston Churchill or Rudyard Kipling.

See Plate No. 133 for a letter from Lord Kitchener.

See Plate No. 317 for Lord Robert's signature.

OFFICIAL DOCUMENTS AND ANNOUNCEMENTS

This is an enormous field. Under this category fall all the official documents issued by all the governments of all the nations who participated in the Boer War. By looking at the home countries of the contingents represented in the war one will gain an idea of the amount of paper that was issued to move troops, ships, ammunition and supplies, nurses, ambulances, horses, mail and so on.
These items can be collected in many, many countries.

Plate 317
Top Row: Official documents.
A 'Royal Sussex Regiment' booklet.
A paybook issued by the Royal Sussex Regiment of Infantry to Ernest Packham.

Bottom Row: Signature of Lord Roberts.
A religious publication called *A Christian Colour-Sergeant — Brief Memoir of Col-Sergt. Macmillan — Black Watch who fell at Magersfontein on 11th Dec. 1899*.
'The Small Book' issued by the Army Service Corps to W. J. Ryan carrying his description and attestation, next-of-kin, promotions, campaigns and actions, medals, good conduct pay, etc.
(From the Oosthuizen Collection)

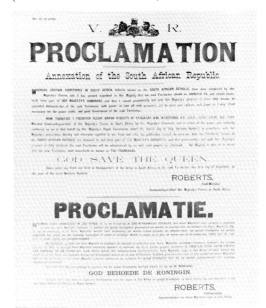

Plate 318
One of the most famous official announcements — The Proclamation announcing the 'Annexation of the South African Republic' and renaming the territory 'The Transvaal'.
(From the Oosthuizen Collection)

MISCELLANEOUS EPHEMERA
Plate 319
A folding sheet, on the front the title 'The Absent-Minded Beggar' by Rudyard Kipling

172 Boer War Memorabilia

319 with a photographic picture of Kipling. Folded open it contains the four verses of the poem with the sketch 'A Gentleman in Kharki' by R. Caton Woodville in the centre. On the back the words 'The whole proceeds from the sale of this poem will be devoted by the *Daily Mail* in the name of Rudyard Kipling to the benefit of the wives and children of the Reservists'.
(24 × 12½ in. – 61 × 31.8 cm.)
(*From the collection of Mr Kenneth Griffith, London*)

320

Plate 320
A nine-picture fan made of stiff card with fabric reinforcement. It is printed in three shades of green with the figures of 'A Gentleman in Kharki', MacDonald, French, White, Roberts, Buller, Kitchener, Baden-Powell and 'The Handy Man' in black.
(9¾ in. – 24.7 cm. open 14¾ in. – 36.7 cm.)
(*By courtesy of Rita & Ian Smythe, Britannia, London*)

Plate 321
Figure 1: A Red Cross identity card carried by most of the Boer soldiers at the beginning of the war.
Figure 2: 'Fall of Pretoria'. A folder containing the texts of pro-British songs (no music).
Figure 3: A copy of an 'Official Programme' of the march through London of the City Imperial Volunteers on their 'Triumphal Return' on 27th October 1900.
Figure 4: A permit issued by the Diyatalawa POW Camp for a visitor to enter the camp.
(*From the collection of Mr Kenneth Griffith, London*)

Ephemera

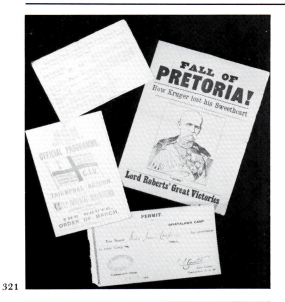

Plate 323
A souvenir of the visit of President Kruger to France in his efforts to obtain assistance in Europe to save his country.
(*By courtesy of the National Cultural History and Open-Air Museum, Pretoria*)

Plate 322
A programme of Boer songs and live scenes performed at the Halleschen Stadttheater in Germany on 10th 11th and 12th May 1902.
(*By courtesy of the National Cultural History and Open-Air Museum, Pretoria*)

Plate 324
A copy of the programme of the New Year's Concert given by the Boers' Music Society in the POW Camp in Dyatalawa, Ceylon, Tuesday 31st December 1901.
(*By courtesy of the National Cultural History and Open-Air Museum, Pretoria*)

Plate 325
'*Den Helden*' (The Heroes) a pro-Boer poem in German written by Wilhelm Küpfer in Santiago, Chile.
(*By courtesy of the National Cultural History and Open-Air Museum, Pretoria*)

Plate 326
'*Ter Gedachtenis*' (In Memory) certificates issued in different forms by Boer commandants to their fellow soldiers commemorating their participation in the Boer War.
(*By courtesy of the National Cultural History and Open-Air Museum, Pretoria*)

Plate 327
A Dutch cardboard chocolate box with a photograph of General Joubert and the wording 'Generaal Piet Joubert 'sRademakers Chocolade', 'Rademakers Chocolade 'sRademakers Cacao' and '*Eendragt Maakt Magt*' (unity is strength).
(*By courtesy of the War Museum of the Boer Republics, Bloemfontein*)

Plate 328
Figure 1: 'Dollar' cigarette packet. These cigarettes were sent to the British troops in South Africa during the Boer War. A notice printed on the packet reads: 'To the Soldiers of the King'.

Figure 2: 'Krüger Arroz', cigarettes, made in Las Palmas and purchased by British troops in transit to and from South Africa.
(*By courtesy of the War Museum of the Boer Republics, Bloemfontein*)

Plate 329
A caricature of President Kruger sitting below two pictures of the Hon. J. Chamberlain.
(7 × 7 in. – 17.8 × 17.8 cm.)
(*By courtesy of the War Museum of the Boer Republics, Bloemfontein*)

CHAPTER 11

Textiles

A number of items in the textile field are of interest to collectors. Many general items — embroideries, cloths, bedspreads and a great number of ties and belts — were produced in the prisoner-of-war camps in South Africa and overseas.

In the internment camps (later called concentration camps) in South Africa the women spent much of their time making clothing for the children and also made many a fine piece of embroidery.

In the United Kingdom a great variety of silk and cotton handkerchiefs were made, some small, some very large, honouring military events and personalities. Many of the battles regiments participated in were also commemorated on handkerchiefs and scarves. Flags or white truce flags (some carrying signatures) are also extensively collected.
Stevengraphs with Boer War themes are also collected and the items still appear regularly at auctions and in antique stores. Mr Thomas Stevens invented the 'Stevengraph' — a technique for weaving pictures in pure silk. Mr Stevens' factory, the Stevengraph Works, was in Coventry. He started to produce his multi-coloured silk pictures on book-markers, and subsequently produced a variety of cards, sashes and badges. The following 'Stevengraphs' were produced by the Stevengraph Works and would be of interest to collectors of Boer War memorabilia.

The late Queen Victoria
King Edward VII
Queen Alexandra
Right Hon. Joseph Chamberlain MP
Right Hon. W. E. Gladstone MP
Lord Roberts
Lord Kitchener
General Buller
General Baden-Powell
General MacDonald
General French
The late General Wauchope
'A Gentleman in Kharki'

Another producer of 'Stevengraphs' was the firm of W. H. Grant, and they were also manufactured by a number of European weavers. One was produced with the picture of President Kruger.

178 Boer War Memorabilia

Plate 330
A selection of Stevengraphs.

Top row
Figure 1: With a picture of Lord Roberts with the wording 'Empire Makers', 'For Queen and Country', 'Woven in pure silk' and 'Field Marshal Lord Roberts V.C.'.
(7 × 5 in. – 17.8 × 12.6 cm.)
Figure 2: With a picture of General Buller with the wording 'Empire Makers', 'Ladysmith Feby 28th 1900', 'Woven in pure silk' and 'Sir Redvers Buller V.C.'.
(7 × 5 in. – 17.8 × 12.6 cm.)

Bottom row
Figure 1: With a picture of General Wauchope and the wording 'A Scottish Hero', 'Maj-Gen Wauchope C.B.', '(Killed in Action)', 'Magersfontein — Dec 11th 1899' and 'Woven in pure silk'.
(7 × 5 in. – 17.8 × 12.6 cm.)
Figure 2: With a picture of a soldier with the wording 'R. Caton Woodville 1899' and 'A Gentleman in Kharki'.
(7 × 5 in. – 17.8 × 12.6 cm.)
Figure 3: A picture of Gladstone with the wording 'Tried, Trusted, True', 'Woven in pure silk' and 'Right Hon. W. E. Gladstone M.P.'.
(Mr Gladstone's Conventions endeavoured to arrange a settlement of the Transvaal issue after the 1st Boer War.)
($7\frac{5}{16} \times 5\frac{7}{16}$ in. – 18.6 × 13.8 cm.)
(*From the Oosthuizen Collection*)

Plate 331
A Stevengraph with a picture of Lord Kitchener with the wording 'Kitchener of Khartoum' and 'Egypt — Soudan 1898 — South Africa 1899–1900'.
(Woven in pure silk by T. Stevens, Coventry)
(*By permission of the National Army Museum, London*)

Plate 332
A Stevengraph with a picture of Major-General Baden-Powell with the wording 'Baden Powell' and 'Prince of Scouts & Hero of Mafeking'.
(Woven in pure silk by T. Stevens, Coventry)
(*By permission of the National Army Museum, London*)

Plate 333
A German 'Stevengraph' with a picture of President Kruger with the wording '*Präsident Krüger*'.
(5 × 3 in. – 12.7 × 7.6 cm.)
(*By courtesy of the War Museum of the Boer Republics, Bloemfontein*)

Textiles 179

332

333

334

Plate 334
A 'Stevengraph' of a seated President Kruger with the wording '*Geweef in Zijde*' (Woven in silk), '*Präsident Krüger*' and '*Eendracht maakt Macht*' (unity is strength).
(*By courtesy of the War Museum of the Boer Republics, Bloemfontein*)

Plate 335
A selection of handkerchiefs with Boer War themes:

Figure 1: A handkerchief in the form of a Union Jack flag with a medallion picture of 'Lord Roberts V.C.' surrounded with the names 'Pretoria, Ladysmith, Elandslaagte, Mafeking, Spionkop, Colenso, Belmont, Bloemfontein, Rensburg, Colesberg, Pietershill, Dreifontein, Paardeberg and Kimberley'.
(27 × 29 in. – 68.6 × 73.6 cm.)
Figure 2: A silk handkerchief with a list of the 'Engagements of 1st Battn. Essex Regiment'.
(22 × 21 in. – 55.9 × 53.3 cm.)
Figure 3: A handkerchief with the A.B.C.: 'A Stands for Army, etc., etc.
(15 × 16 in. – 38.1 × 40.6 cm.)

Figure 2: A handkerchief entitled 'The Absent-Minded Beggar' with the poem by Rudyard Kipling and the music by Arthur Sullivan, pictures of Lord Roberts and Queen Victoria, 'God Save the Queen', and a map of the South African Republic and the Orange Free State.

$(17\frac{1}{4} \times 16\frac{3}{4}$ in. $- 43.8 \times 42.5$ cm.)
(From the Oosthuizen Collection)

Figure 4: A handkerchief with a picture in the centre entitled 'The Last Cartridge' surrounded with pictures of 'Lord Roberts, Rt. Hon. J. Chamberlain M.P., Sir George White V.C., President Kruger and General Joubert'.

$(13 \times 12\frac{5}{8}$ in. $- 33 \times 32$ cm.)

Figure 5: A silk handkerchief with a list of the 'Engagements of Gen. Sir Redvers Buller's Natal Field Forces'.

$(20\frac{1}{2} \times 20$ in. $— 52 \times 50.8$ cm.)

Figure 6: A handkerchief in the form of a Union Jack flag with a round picture of Lord Roberts entitled 'Bobs' and 'Kimberley, Ladysmith, Bloemfontein, Brandfort, Kroonstad, Mafeking, The Vaal and Pretoria'.

$(33 \times 28\frac{3}{4}$ in. $- 83.8 \times 73$ cm.)
(From the Oosthuizen Collection)

Plate 336

Figure 1: A handkerchief with a 'Map of the Transvaal' and two oval pictures of 'President Stephen John Paul Kruger' and 'The Right Hon. Joseph Chamberlain'.

$(25\frac{1}{2} \times 24$ in. $- 64.8 \times 61$ cm.)

Plate 337
A handkerchief with a picture of Lord Roberts with the wording 'India 1879–1893 — South Africa 1900 Lord Roberts of Kandahar'.

$(24 \times 24$ in. $- 61 \times 61$ cm.)
(By permission of the Africana Museum, Johannesburg)

Textiles 181

Plate 338
A handkerchief with a picture of Lord Roberts surrounded with pictures of other generals with the title 'United We Stand for Queen and Empire'.
(12 × 15 in. – 30.5 × 38.1 cm.)
(*By permission of the Africana Museum, Johannesburg*)

Plate 340
A handkerchief with a centre picture of the 'Earl of Albemarle Commander of Infantry Division' and in the surrounding panels the following: 'C.I.V.', 'Souvenir of London Volunteers Left London January 13th First time in Action Jacobsdal February 16th' and 'An escort of the C.I.V. accompanied General Cronje to Cape Town'.
(*By permission of the National Army Museum, London*)

Plate 339
A handkerchief with the 'Declaration of Peace Anglo-Boer War 1899–1902'.
(10 × 18 in. – 25.4 × 45.7 cm.)
(*By permission of the Africana Museum, Johannesburg*)

Plate 341
A handkerchief with the 'Engagements of XVIII Hussars South Africa'.
(*By permission of the National Army Museum, London*)

Plate 342
A handkerchief with 'Incidents in the Transvaal War' and 'British Hoisting the Union Jack at Pretoria'.
(By permission of the National Army Museum, London)

Plate 344
Lord Robert's Johannesburg Proclamation printed in gold on a silk Union Jack.
(By permission of the Africana Museum, Johannesburg)

Plate 343
A handkerchief with a picture of 'Gen. Sir Redvers Buller V.C. G.C.B. K.C.M.G' and the words 'The Colonies Rally Round the Old Flag of England', and pictures of the following: Queensland Mounted Rifles; South Australian Lancers; Cape Mounted Rifles; New South Wales Lancers; Hong Kong Volunteer Corps; Australian Infantry; Cape Town Highlander; Canadian Rifleman; The Motor Gun Carriage.
(By permission of the National Army Museum, London)

Plate 345
A linen cloth with the signatures of Boer prisoners of war in the Diyatalawa Camp in Ceylon, with the coat-of-arms of the South African Republic in the centre with the wording 'Boercamp Diyatalawa Ceylon 1900–1902' and '*Uns zieht der Reumathismus fürs Transvaal auch durch's Kreuz*'.
(36 × 36 in. – 91.5 × 91.5 cm.)
(By permission of the Africana Museum, Johannesburg)

Textiles 183

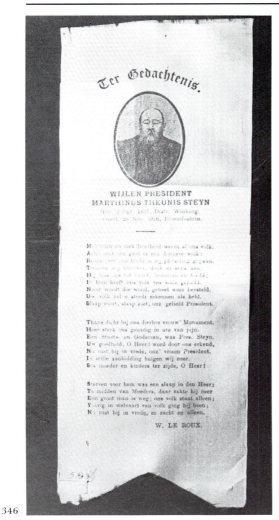

Plate 346
A silk bookmark in memory of President Steyn with a poem by W. le Roux lamenting his passing.
(*By courtesy of the War Museum of the Boer Republics, Bloemfontein*)

Plate 347
A patchwork cloth made by a Mrs R. W. Keet of Ermelo, started in 1900 and completed 'April 14, 1902' with two crossed Transvaal flags in the centre.
(42 × 17½ in. – 106.7 × 44.5 cm.)
(*By courtesy of the National Cultural History and Open-Air Museum, Pretoria*)

Plate 348
A cloth with the embroidered signatures of internees. The coat-of-arms of the Transvaal is in the centre and the Transvaal and Orange Free State flags are in the top corners.
(*By courtesy of the National Cultural History and Open-Air Museum, Pretoria*)

Plate 349
Figure 1: A silk bookmark with the wording 'V.R. S.A. Kimberley relieved Feb. 16, 1900 Ladysmith Feb. 28 Mafeking May 17 Praise ye the Lord'.

Figure 2: A small cross-stich embroidery with the words: 'Boer M.H. War'.
$(4\frac{1}{2} \times 4\frac{1}{2}$ in. – 11.4 × 11.4 cm.)

Figure 3: A Singer's Bookmark advertisement for a silk picture of Major-General J. D. P. French, born 1852.
(*From the Oosthuizen Collection*)

Plate 350
An embroidered cloth made during the Siege of Ladysmith, with the words 'Siege of Ladysmith 1st Nov.r 1899 28th Feb.y 1900 120 days'.
(36 × 36 in. – 91.5 × 91.5 cm.)
(*By permission of the Africana Museum, Johannesburg*)

Plate 351
A silk cover for Queen Victoria's 'Chocolate Tin' gift to the troops.
On the front: A medal with a picture of Queen Victoria and a picture of Empire soldiers with their chocolate gift tins.
On the reverse: A six-verse poem by Riche Ossulston-Rich called 'My present from the Queen'.
(*By courtesy of Mr Kenneth Griffith, London*)

Plate 352
A shoulder band (sash) and a rosette in the colours of the Orange Free State Republic.
(*By courtesy of the War Museum of the Boer Republics, Bloemfontein*)

Plate 353
A shoulder band (sash) in the colours of the Orange Free State with its coat-of-arms.
(*By courtesy of the War Museum of the Boer Republics, Bloemfontein*)

Plate 354
A shoulder band (sash) with the Transvaal colours and a button with a picture of President Kruger.
(*By permission of the National Army Museum, London*)

Textiles 185

353

355

354

356

Plate 355
A shoulder band (sash) in the colours of the South African Republic with its coat-of-arms.
(*By permission of the National Army Museum, London*)

Plate 356
A tapestry of 'M. G. Baden Powell' with his picture in the centre.
(*By courtesy of The Scout Association, Baden-Powell House, London*)

186 Boer War Memorabilia

357

Plate 357
A tapestry made by A. Willette depicting President Kruger in exile, with a Dutch girl. About forty of these tapestries were woven and sold to raise funds.
(2 × 3 ft. – 61 × 91.5 cm.)
(*By courtesy of the National Cultural History and Open-Air Museum, Pretoria*)

Plate 358
A tapestry made in Germany in 1900, depicting General C.R.de Wet, an armoured train and other scenes from the Boer War. (tablecloth size).
(*By courtesy of the War Museum of the Boer Republics, Bloemfontein*)

with the words '*Dem Heldenvolk and seinen Führern*' (To the heroic people and their leaders). (6 ft. 6 in. high – 198.2 cm.)
(*By courtesy of the War Museum of the Boer Republics, Bloemfontein*)

Plate 360
A German banner in the form of the flag and coat-of-arms of the Orange Free State, embroidered with the words '*Dem Heldenvolk und seinen Führern*' (To the heroic people and their leaders). (6 ft. 6 in. high – 198.2 cm.)
(*By courtesy of the War Museum of the Boer Republics, Bloemfontein*)

Plate 359
A German banner in the form of the flag and coat-of-arms of the Transvaal, embroidered

CHAPTER 12

General

Books, medallions, trench souvenirs, knives, ashtrays, umbrella stands, tables, pipes, lapel pins, trivets, viewers and miscellaneous items

BOOKS
The collecting of Boer War books is an extensive field and will not be covered in this book on memorabilia. In this chapter, attention will only be given to unusual books, or books which have caught the attention of collectors because of their treatment of a specific item, an attractive cover or the coverage of an unusual topic.

There are excellent books on the market covering all aspects of the Boer War in great detail and one or two new publications come on to the market annually. It is still relatively easy to find the older publications on the shelves of bookshops and dealers specializing in the specific field of history or militaria.

Plate 361
Examples of some of the unusual and interesting books published.

Top left: *The Transvaal War* published by *The Illustrated London News*. A colourful description of the war with photographs and good etchings and also interesting Boer War advertisements.

Top right: *Celebrities of the Army 1900* published by George Newnes Ltd., London, with colourful photographs of most of the key officers who participated in the Boer War. The extract is the photograph of 'Lieutenant-Colonel F. L. Lessard, Canadian Mounted Infantry, South Africa'. On the back of each photograph is also a brief description of the officer's career.
These photographs were also published and sold individually.

Bottom left: *With the Flag to Pretoria*: Volumes I and II were published by Harmsworth Bros. Ltd. from the magazines *With the Flag to Pretoria*. Different colours were used for the cover.

Bottom right: *The Tremendous Twins, or How the Boers were beaten*. An amusing children's book of verses and coloured drawings. The pictures by Mrs Ernest Ames, the verses by Ernest Ames.
(*From the Oosthuizen Collection*)

MEDALS/MEDALLIONS

There are a number of definitive works on service medals and also on Boer War medallions. This chapter will endeavour to give the reader an overview of the various kinds of commemorative medals which were issued.

361

Plates 363 and 364
A silver medallion.

Side 1: 'To the memory of those who gave their lives for Queen and Country' and 'South African Campaign 1899–1900'.

Side 2: 'Pax' (3 in. – 7 cm.)
(*From the Oosthuizen Collection*)

Plate 362
Two interesting collectors' pieces.

Figure 1. 'Sketches in Mafeking & East Africa' by Major-General R. S. S. Baden-Powell.

Figure 2. 'Siege Views Mafeking' from original photos by E. J. Ross taken during the Siege.
(*By courtesy of The Scout Association, Baden-Powell House, London*)

Plates 365 and 366
A silver metal medallion.

Side 1: 'Lent to British Govt for use in Transvaal War by Pres. of Atlanta Transport Coy.' and 'S.S. Maine Bernard N. Baker Esq. 1899'.

Side 2: 'For the American Ladies Hospital Ship Fund. Chairman Lady R. Churchill Hon. Sec. Mrs. A. Blow Hon. Tres. Mrs. Ronalds' and 'Fitted as Hospital Ship by Messrs. Fletcher Son & Fearnall Ltd. London'. ($1\frac{3}{4}$ in. – 4.4 cm.)
(*From the Oosthuizen Collection*)

362

Plates 367 and 368
A silver medallion.

Side 1: 'Lord Roberts'.

Side 2: '1900 Bloemfontein Pretoria'.
(*By permission of the National Army Museum, London*)

363

364

365

366

367

368

Plates 369 and 370
A bronze pendant-medallion.

Side 1: 'Field Marshal Roberts of Kandahar'.

Side 2: 'Society of Miniature Rifle-Clubs'.
(1⅛ in. – 2.8 cm.)
(*From the Oosthuizen Collection*)

Plates 371 and 372
Mounted 'British Empire Medal'.

Side 1: 'South Africa virtute et ductu pax quaeritur bello 1901'
(with Lord Roberts).

Side 2: 'Oppressorum Conservator Edward VII D. G. Rex et I' and 'Transvaal & Orange River Colonies'.
(*By permission of the National Army Museum, London*)

Plate 373
A Canadian enamel and silver medal.
'In Honor of our Absent Minded Beggars in South Africa', 'England', 'Canada'.
(*By permission of the National Army Museum, London*)

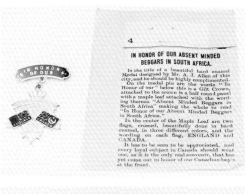

373

374

375

376

377

Plates 376 and 377
A Canadian medallion.

Side 1: 'Canada In South Africa 1899–1900 For Crown & Empire'.

Side 2: 'T.R.H. The Duke & Duchess of Cornwall & York visited Canada 1901'.
(*By permission of the National Army Museum, London*)

Plates 378 and 379
This medallion is a token of the Commonwealth Unity of Great Britain and Australia.

Side 1: 'United in the cause of freedom' 'We serve under one crown' 'We defend one empire'.

Plates 374 and 375
A silver metal medallion.

Side 1: 'F. M. Lord Roberts V.C.'
Side 2: 'Pretoria 1900'.
(*By permission of the National Army Museum, London*)

194 Boer War Memorabilia

378

380

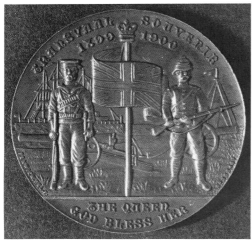

379

381

Side 2: 'Transvaal souvenir 1899 1900', 'The Queen God bless her'.
(*By permission of the National Army Museum, London*)

Plates 380 and 381
The C.I.V. medallion.

Side 1: 'The City of London Imperial Volunteers raised and equipped for the War in South Africa by the Citizens of London. Formed December 1899 Returned to London October 1900'.

Side 2: 'Pro Patria Regina et Urbe'.
(*By permission of the National Army Museum, London*)

382

Plates 382 and 383
The Newark Medallion.

Side 1: 'Borough of Newark 1900 Appleby, Mayor'.

Side 2: 'Struck in aid of the Mayor's Fund for the Families of Newark Soldiers who fought in the Transvaal War'.
(*By courtesy of the National Army Museum, London*)

Side 2: 'S. Africa 1899–1900', 'Gen. Baden-Powell', 'Lord Roberts V.C.' and 'General French'.
(*By courtesy of the National Army Museum, London*)

Plates 384 and 385
The Kings Lynn medallion.

Side 1: 'A Souvenir of South African War 1899–1900 Kings Lynn' and 'George Bristow Mayor'.

Plates 386 and 387
The St. John's Medallion.

Side 1: 'Magnus Prioratus Ordinis Hospitalis Sancti Johannis Jerusalem in Anglia' and 'South Africa 1899–1902'.

Side 2: 'Edwardus VII D.G. Britt. Rex F.D. Ind. Imp.'.
(*By permission of the National Army Museum, London*)

387

388

Plate 388

Figure 1: Boer with gun inscribed '*Alles zal recht kom*' (All will be well). On the back a calf on an altar inscribed: '*God behoede Land en Volk 1899–1900*' (God bless land and nation).
($1\frac{1}{16}$ in. – 2.7 cm.)

Figure 2: Bronze medal inscribed: 'S. J. P. Kruger, *Staatspresident der Z.A. Republiek 1883–1900*' (State President of the S.A. Republic). On the back: '*Volkstem-Aandenking Begrafenis van de grote Afrikaner* Paul Kruger Pretoria Dec 1904' (Volkstem-Newspaper commemorative of Funeral of the great Afrikaner Paul Kruger).
($1\frac{1}{8}$ in. – 2.8 cm.)

Figure 3: Dutch medal with a burning Boer farm house inscribed '1899–1901 *De Engelschen in Zuid Afrika*' '*Dan voor een geveinsde vrede te worden bedrogen*' (The English in South Africa — Then to be cheated by a sham peace).
($1\frac{5}{16}$ in. – 3.3 cm.)
(*From the Oosthuizen Collection*)

389

390

Plates 389 and 390
A bronze medallion.

Side 1: 'Paul Krüger President der Zuid Afrikaansche Republiek 10 Oct. 1825'.

Side 2: '*Aan de dappere Strijders voor Recht en Vrijheid* 1899–1900' (To the brave fighters for right and freedom).   ($1\frac{1}{2}$ in. – 3.8 cm.)
(*From the Oosthuizen Collection*)

General 197

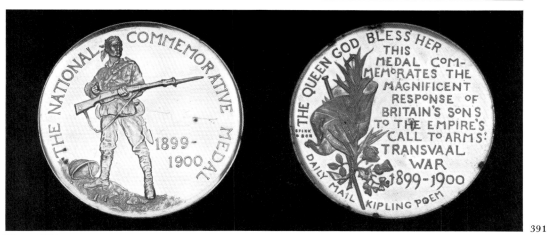

Plate 391
The 'Absent-Minded Beggar' medal. Struck by Spink & Son. Part of the price of this bronze-gilt medal was given to the proprietors of the *Daily Mail* for the Kipling Poem War Fund.

Side 1: 'The National Commemorative Medal 1899–1900'.

Side 2: 'The Queen God Bless Her', 'This medal commemorates the magnificent response of Britain's Sons to the Empire's call to arms. Transvaal War 1899–1900', '*Daily Mail* — Kipling Poem'.

($1\frac{3}{4}$ in. – 4.5 cm.)

(*From the Oosthuizen Collection*)

Plate 392

Figure 1: A bronze plaque inscribed 'President Krüger' and '*Eendragt Maakt Magt*' (unity is strength).

($2 \times 1\frac{9}{16}$ in. – 5.1 × 4 cm.)

Figure 2: A silver metal plaque inscribed: 'A Gentleman in Kharki 1899–1900' and 'Transvaal War'.

($2\frac{1}{4} \times 1\frac{1}{2}$ in. – 5.7 × 3.8 cm.)

(*From the Oosthuizen Collection*)

393

394

395

Side 2: 'Colenso 15e December 1889'.
(*By courtesy of the National Cultural History and Open-Air Museum, Pretoria*)

396

Plate 396
A medallion issued in nickel and bronze.

Side 1: 'Christian de Wet' 'Koos de la Reij'.

Side 2: 'Hands Off!' '1902'.
(*By courtesy of the National Cultural History and Open-Air Museum, Pretoria*)

Plates 393 and 394
A bronze medallion.

Side 1: 'M. T. Steijn Staatspres. van den Oranje-Vrijstaat' (M. T. Steijn State Pres. of the Orange Free State).

Side 2: 'Verwond maar niet verwonnen' (Wounded but not conquered).
$(2\frac{3}{8}$ in. -6 cm.$)$
(*From the Oosthuizen Collection*)

Plate 395
A medallion issued in silver and bronze.

Side 1: 'L. Botha' (General Botha).

397

Plate 397
A six-sided medallion of President Kruger inscribed 'Paul Kruger'.
(*By courtesy of the National Cultural History and Open-Air Museum, Pretoria*)

Plate 398
A medallion made by POWs in St. Helena and issued to winners of sporting events. Inscription '*Republikeinsche Sport Vereeniging* St. Helena 1900' (Republican Sport Association).
(*By courtesy of the National Cultural History and Open-Air Museum, Pretoria*)

MILITARY ITEMS AND MILITARIA
Collecting militaria is a very large and specialized field and cannot be covered in a chapter or two.

However, any collectors of Boer War memorabilia very often also collect military items ranging from weapons and uniforms to food containers.

AMMUNITION FRAGMENTS
Ammunition fragments collected by soldiers later became known by the name of 'Trench Souvenirs' or 'Trench Art'.

Plate 399
A brass brooch made from a Boer shell. It is engraved '4/2/1901 T'.
(*By permission of the National Army Museum, London*)

Plate 400

Back row

Figure 1: A matchholder and striker with a small plaque marked 'From the Teak of H.M.S. *Terrible* whose guns relieved Ladysmith'. ($2\frac{1}{4}$ in. – 5.7 cm.)

Figure 2: A wooden money box with a small plaque marked 'From the Teak of H.M.S. *Terrible* whose guns relieved Ladysmith'. ($3\frac{1}{4}$ in. – 8.3 cm.)

Figure 3: A cannon fragment on a wood base with a silver plaque with the inscription 'Lindley 1900'.
(height $3\frac{1}{2}$ in. – 8.9 cm., base $4\frac{1}{2}$ in. – 11.5 cm.)

Figure 4: A cannon fragment mounted on a wooden base with a silver plaque with the engraving 'Ladysmith 1899 – 1900'. ($3\frac{1}{2}$ in. – 8.9 cm.)

Figure 5: A shell and bullet turned into a pocket knife with the engraving 'To Chas. Steele from W. H. Lee Sgt. Boer War 1899 – 1900'. ($3\frac{1}{8}$ in. – 8 cm.)

Front row

Figure 1: A wooden matcholder with the inscription 'From the Teak of H.M.S. *Terrible* whose guns relieved Ladysmith'. ($2\frac{1}{4}$ in. – 5.7 cm.)

Figure 2: A cannon fragment with a silver handle with the engraving 'Siege of Kimberley 14th Oct. 1899 15th Feb. 1900'. (3 in. – 7.6 cm.)

Figure 3: A copper knife-rest with the engraving 'Band of 94 Pounder Mafeking Siege'. ($3\frac{1}{2}$ in. – 8.9 cm.)

Figure 4: A shell casing with the words 'Pom Pom Shell Bloemfontein Boer War S. Africa 1899'. ($3\frac{3}{4}$ in. – 9.5 cm.)
(*Items 2 and 3 from the front row by courtesy of Mr Kenneth Griffith, London; the remaining items from the Oosthuizen Collection*)

400

KNIVES, ETC
Most soldiers carried pockets knives, many of which became collectors' items. Some carry names and initials, while others are unmarked.

There were also scissors made with Boer War figures etched on them.

401

Plate 401
A knife popular with the Boer soldiers. Knives of this type, made in Germany, were manufactured in different-coloured metals.
On the front: The pictures of 'Krüger' and 'De Wet'.
On the back: The coats-of-arms of the Transvaal and the Orange Free State and the words 'Transvaal — *Eendracht maakt macht* (unity is strength) — Orange Freist.'

(3½ in. – 8.9 cm.)

(*From the Oosthuizen Collection*)

Plate 402
A pair of scissors with the picture of President Kruger etched where the blades join.
(*By permission of the Africana Museum, Johannesburg*)

ASHTRAYS
Ashtrays have always been popular with collectors in general. During the Boer War ashtrays were made from shells, from silver (*see* Chapter 8) and also in other metals (*see* Chapter 9).

402

Plate 403

Figure 1: A brass ashtray with a picture of 'Field Marshal Lord Roberts' impressed in the centre. ($4\frac{1}{2}$ in. – 10.8 cm.)

Figure 2: A copper ashtray with a picture of Lord Roberts and the words 'South Africa' in the centre. On the rim the pictures and names of the following generals: 'Kitchener. White, French, Kekewich, Warren, Rundle, Plumer, Clery, Kelly-Kenny, Methuen, MacDonald, Baden-Powell, Buller.' ($4\frac{3}{4}$ in. – 12.1 cm.)

(From the Oosthuizen Collection)

MATCH COVERS

Although vestas were very popular at the turn of the century, covers were also made for match boxes.

UMBRELLA STANDS

Cast-iron umbrella stands are of interest to the collectors of Boer War memorabilia

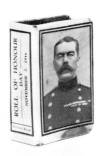

Plate 404

Figure 1: On the front pictures of Lord Kitchener and General French. On the reverse the words: 'Kitchener, French & Co. Great Britain Map Revising Specialists. Large Staff of Trained Men always ready for service in any part of the Globe. UNLIMITED vacancies open for energetic young men.' ($2\frac{1}{4} \times 1\frac{5}{8}$ in. – 5.7 × 4.1 cm.)

Figure 2: On the front a picture of Lord Kitchener. On the reverse the history of Lord Kitchener from birth to his death. Issued at time of First World War but of general interest to Boer War collectors. ($2\frac{1}{2} \times 1\frac{5}{8}$ in. – 6.4 × 4.2 cm.)

(From the Oosthuizen Collection)

Plate 405

A cast-iron umbrella stand of a British soldier with the words 'The Man in Khaki' embossed at the bottom. (28 in. – 71.1 cm.)
(From the Oosthuizen Collection)

Plate 406

A cast-iron umbrella stand with the figure of Lord Roberts and the embossed word 'Bobs' below the figure. ($29\frac{1}{2}$ in. – 75 cm.)
(From the collection of Mr Kenneth Griffith, London)

Plate 407

A cast-iron umbrella stand with the figure of Major-General Baden-Powell and the letters 'B.P.' on the base.
Manufacturer's mark: Biclam.
(28 in. – 71.1 cm.)
(From the collection of Mr Kenneth Griffith, London)

406

407

TABLES
A number of cast-iron tables were manufactured to honour Boer War generals and events.

408

409

Plate 408

A cast-iron table with a white wooden top with the moulded figure of 'A Gentleman in Kharki' and the names 'Ladysmith', 'Pretoria' and 'Mafeking'.

(height 30 in. – 76.2 cm.
diameter 24 in. – 61 cm.)

(*From the collection of Mr Kenneth Griffith, London*)

Plate 409

A cast-iron table with a wooden top with a moulded figure of Major-General Baden-Powell and the moulded letters 'B.P.'.

(height 29 in. – 73.6 cm.,
diameter $23\frac{1}{2}$ in. – 59.7 cm.)

(*From the collection of Mr Kenneth Griffith, London*)

PIPES AND TAMPERS

Pipe smoking was very popular at the turn of the century. As there were not sufficient pipes available in South Africa to meet the soldiers' demands, a number of campaigns were launched in England and a great number of pipes were collected and shipped to the war front. The soldiers in their leisure time also carved their names or regimental insignia on their pipes. Pipes have thus become another item high on the collectors' lists.

In most of the etchings and caricatures of President Kruger he was portrayed with a pipe in his mouth.

Plate 410

Figure 1: A meerschaum pipe of a soldier with 'C.I.V.' engraved on his hat.
($3\frac{3}{4}$ in. – 9.5 cm.)

Figure 2: A meerschaum pipe of King Edward VII. ($4\frac{7}{8}$ in. – 12.4 cm.)

Figure 3: A brass pipe tamper with the face of Lord Roberts. ($2\frac{1}{2}$ in. – 6.4 cm.)

Figure 4: A meerschaum pipe of General White. ($5\frac{1}{2}$ in. – 14 cm.)

Figure 5: A finely-carved meerschaum pipe of Queen Victoria. On the bowl the engraving '*R. D 'Angletere*'. ($5\frac{1}{2}$ in. – 14 cm.)

(*Figure 2 by courtesy of Mr Brian Tipping, 'The Pipe Shop', Antiquarius, London; other items from the Oosthuizen Collection*)

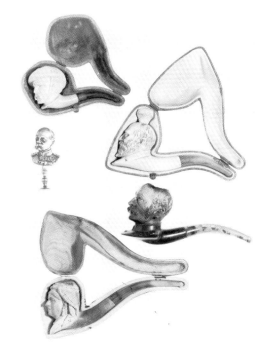

410

Plate 411

Figure 1: A pipe engraved with the crest of the 'Northd Fusrs' and 'Transvaal 1899 – 1900 – 1901 L.De.H.L.'.
($6\frac{1}{4}$ in. – 15.9 cm.)

Figure 2: A pipe engraved with a crest: 'South Stafford' and 'Boer — 1900 — War' 'South Africa'. ($6\frac{1}{2}$ in. – 16.5 cm.)

Figure 3: This pipe has engraved on it the ZAR (South African Republic) coat-of-arms and the motto '*Eendracht maakt magt*' (unity is strength) and the following: 'Boer War', '1899 – 1902' and 'From Percy to Will'.
($6\frac{1}{4}$ in. – 15.9 cm.)

Figure 4: POW handicraft. This pipe has engraved on it the coat-of-arms of Great Britain, '*Dieu et Mon Droit*' and 'Cut by F. Petersen P.O.W. Kaity India' '1902'.
(7 in. – 17.8 cm.)

(*The above from the Oosthuizen Collection*)

411

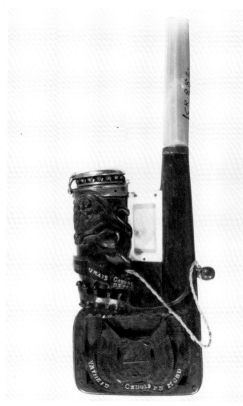

412

Figure 5: A brass and wood pipe rack. Engraved on the brass a picture of the Hospital Ship *Nile*, two crossed flags and '1900'. (7¼ × 6 in. – 18.4 × 15.2 cm.)
(*From the collection of Mr Kenneth Griffith, London*)

Plate 412

This pipe was a gift from Queen Wilhelmina to President Kruger. In the frame behind the bowl is a photograph of Queen Wilhelmina. Engraved on one side is the coat-of-arms of the South African Republic and the motto '*Eendracht maakt macht*' and on the other the coat-of-arms of the Orange Free State and the motto '*Vryheid Geduld en Moed*'.
(*By courtesy of the National Cultural History and Open-Air Museum, Pretoria*)

Plate 413

Figure 1: A German porcelain pipe with a picture of General P. J. Joubert.

Figure 2: A German porcelain pipe with a picture of President Kruger.
(*Photographs by courtesy of Sotheby's, Johannesburg*)

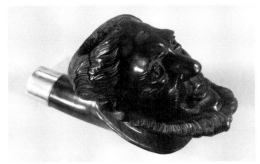

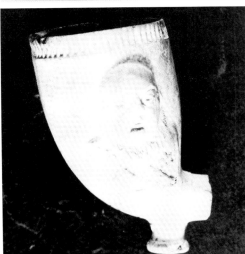

Plate 414
A clay pipe bowl with the image of President Kruger.
(By permission of the National Army Museum, London)

Plate 415
A carved wooden pipe in the image of President Kruger.
(By courtesy of the Douwe Egberts Museum, Utrecht)

Plate 416
A porcelain pipe with a picture of President Kruger in exile.
(By courtesy of the National Cultural History and Open-Air Museum, Pretoria)

206 Boer War Memorabilia

Plate 417
A General Buller clay pipe bowl.
(*By permission of the National Army Museum, London*)

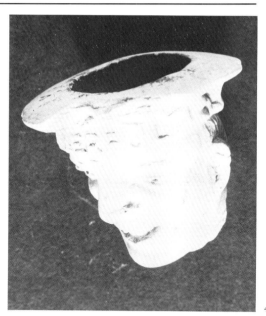

Plate 419
A clay pipe bowl with a rating from the H.M.S. Powerful.
(*By permission of the National Army Museum, London*)

Plate 418
A clay pipe bowl with the image of Lord Roberts and the word 'Bobs'.
(*By permission of the National Army Museum, London*)

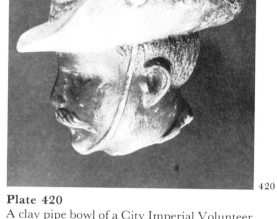

Plate 420
A clay pipe bowl of a City Imperial Volunteer with 'C.I.V.' marked on his hat.
(*By permission of the National Army Museum, London*)

General 207

Plate 421
A stone pipe, carved in the likeness of President Kruger.
(*By courtesy of the War Museum of the Boer Republics, Bloemfontein*)

LAPEL PINS AND BUTTONS
The events of the Boer War created a great deal of excitement. Manufacturers in Great Britain and in Europe made and sold a great number of lapel pins and buttons to cash in on the feelings of the population.

Plate 422
A collection of pro-Boer lapel pins issued during the Boer War.
The two Boer Republic flags, 'Pro-Boer' and Transvaal flag.
'Pro-Boer' button with the flags.
The two Boer Republic flags and the wording '*1899 Eere wien eere toekomt 1900*' (Glory to those deserving glory).
Pictures of General De Wet, General Botha and General Delarey.
(*By courtesy of the National Cultural History and Open-Air Museum, Pretoria*)

Plate 423
Lapel pins in various sizes.
General Buller, Lord Kitchener.
Lord Methuen, Queen Victoria, Gen. Kelly-Kenny.
Lord Kitchener, Major-General Baden-Powell, Queen Victoria, President Kruger and The Empire's Tribute to Queen & Defenders National Bazaar May 24 1900 Empress Rooms, Kensington.
General White, Hon. J. Chamberlain, Lord Roberts, Lord Kitchener.
Lord Roberts, Lion with Boer, General French.
(*From the Oosthuizen Collection*)

Plate 424
A collection of 'Boer War' lapel pins.
General White, General French, Lord Kitchener.
Lord Roberts, Lord Methuen, Major-General Baden-Powell.
Queen Alexandra, Kind Edward VII, Queen Victoria.
Queen Alexandra, Welcome Home Gallant C.I.V.s.
(By permission of the National Army Museum, London)

Boer War Memorabilia

425

426

CELLULOID COLLECTIBLES

'A Gentleman in Kharki' and 'The Handy Man' were the two most popular motifs used by the manufacturers of celluloid memorabilia.

Plate 425

An assortment of 'A Gentleman in Kharki' items.
Tot measure, tape measure, card holder, letter opener, bell, bottle cork, and pin cushion.
(*From the Oosthuizen Collection*)

Plate 426

A celluloid figure of 'A Gentleman in Kharki' on a stand.
(*By permission of the National Army Museum, London*)

MISCELLANEOUS BOER WAR COLLECTABLES

Plate 427

A President Kruger doll. (This is a South African copy of a European-made doll.)
(20 in. – 65 cm.)
(*By courtesy of the National Cultural History and Open-Air Museum, Pretoria*)

General 211

Boer War soldier and sailor dolls were also made in Great Britain.

Plate 428
A tiny 'viewer' in the form of a three-legged pot. In the viewer a poster marked 'Famous Generals at the Front South Africa 1900' and the photographs of nine generals.
$(\frac{5}{8}$ in. $- 1.5$ cm.$)$
(From the Oosthuizen Collection)

Plate 429
A viewer with the imprint 'Perfecscope' and viewing cards of the Boer War printed by 'Underwood & Underwood, Publishers New York, London, Toronto-Canada, Ottawa-Kansas' and the Works & Studios of 'Arlington N. J. Littleton N.H., Washington D.C.'.
(From the Oosthuizen Collection)

Plate 430
Figure 1: 'Best English-made Magic Lantern Slides' for Juvenile Lanterns. Views, Comic, Nursery Tales, etc. 12 slides in each box. 'The Transvaal War'
$(6 \times 2 \times 1$ in. $- 15.2 \times 5 \times 2.5$ cm.$)$

Figure 2: 'The Boer War of 1900'. Coloured Lantern Slides.
Chapter 1 'The Boer Invasion of Natal' Price 2/6 per set. (8 slides) with lecture.
$(3\frac{3}{4} \times 3\frac{3}{4} \times 1\frac{1}{4}$ in. $- 9.5 \times 9.5 \times 3.2$ cm.$)$
There are five boxes of slides in the Boer War Series.
(From the collection of Mr Kenneth Griffith, London)

427

428

212   Boer War Memorabilia

429

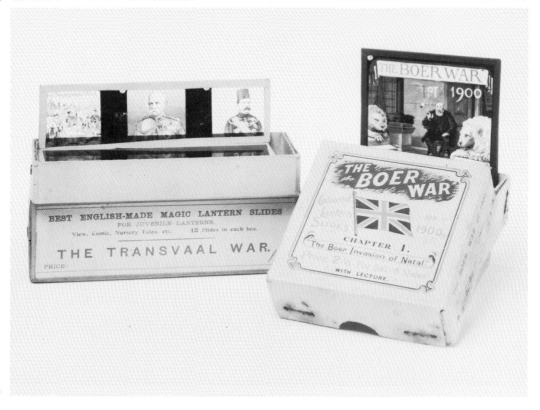

430

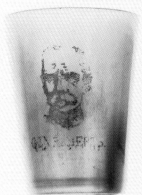

Plate 431

Figure 1: A German-made harmonica impressed 'Cape Town to Pretoria' flanked by pictures of 'Lord Kitchener' and 'Lord Roberts'. On the reverse the trade mark 'M. Hohner'. ($4\frac{5}{8}$ in. – 11.8 cm.)

Figure 2: A small horn cup with a transfer-print picture of 'Gen. Roberts'.
($2\frac{1}{2}$ in. – 6.4 cm.)

Figure 3: A box of Rifleman Pens made by Hinks Wells & Co., Birmingham.
($2\frac{3}{4} \times 2 \times 1$ in. – $7 \times 5.1 \times 2.5$ cm.)
(*From the collection of Mr Kenneth Griffith, London*)

Plate 432

Figure 1: A President Kruger wooden nut-cracker. (8 in. – 20.3 cm.)

Figure 2: A black-painted wooden box with a photograph of President Kruger.
($3 \times 1\frac{5}{8}$ in. – 7.6×4.1 cm.)
(*From the Oosthuizen Collection*)

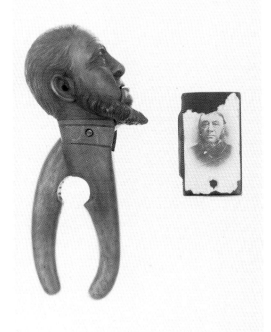

Plate 433
A pair of trivets.

Figure 1: A cast iron trivet with moulded pistols as handle, two crossed swords and a gun, and around the rim the words: 'Britain's might as iron stands'.

(7 in. – 17.8 cm.)

Figure 2: A brass trivet with the figure of and inscription
'A Gentleman in Kharki'.

($8\frac{5}{8}$ in. – 22 cm.)

(*From the Oosthuizen Collection*)

Plate 434
Figure 1: A brass compass engraved: '26th Mx(Cyclist) VCR South Africa 1900 Corp. 1 F. W. Wheeler from Major C. E. Liles'.

($1\frac{3}{4}$ in. – 4.5 cm.)

Figure 2: A brass doorknocker in the image of General French, inscribed 'French'.

($3\frac{1}{2}$ in. – 8.9 cm.)

Figure 3: A brass compass. On the lid the engraving:
'Serg.t A. Potter May 4, 1900'.

(2 in. – 5.1 cm.)

(*From the Oosthuizen Collection*)

Plate 435
Figure 1: A vulcanite vesta with a glazed photograph of Lord Roberts.

($2 \times 1\frac{1}{2}$ in. – 5.1×3.8 cm.)

General 215

Figure 2: A brass paperclip with a picture of 'Lord Roberts'. (1½ in. – 3.8 cm.)

Figure 3: A brass shirt stud with a photograph of 'General Buller'. (⅝ in. – 1.9 cm.)

Figure 4: A brass paperclip with a picture of 'Lord Kitchener'. (½ in. – 1.3 cm.)

Figure 5: An enamelled medallion with a picture of President Kruger. (1 in. – 2.5 cm.)
(*From the Oosthuizen Collection*)

Plate 436
A framed German music box with the figures of Boer generals 'J. H. De-La-Rey' and 'Louis Botha' and the title
 '*Die Helden des Burenkrieges*' (The Heroes of the Boer War).
(18 × 15 in. – 45.7 × 38.1 cm.)
(A similar one was also made with the figures of General De Wet and President Steyn.)
(*By courtesy of the War Museum of the Boer Republics, Bloemfontein*)

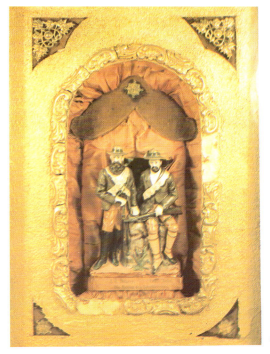

437

Plate 437
A collage in a bottle. On the one side the words: 'In Memory of Great Boer War in South Africa' and on the other side the words: 'By M. J. P. Smidt in the Burgher Refugee Camp, East London'.
(10 in. – 25.4 cm.)
(*By courtesy of the War Museum of the Boer Republics, Bloemfontein*)

Plate 438
A shell-framed picture of General Buller.
(10¾ in. – 27.3 cm.)
(*From the Oosthuizen Collection*)

438

CHAPTER 13

One-of-a-kind Collectables

Presentation caskets, paintings and watercolours, etc.

There are many Boer war collectables which are unique — one of a kind. Excellent examples are the beautiful silver and gold presentation caskets given to generals. Today, these items are usually found in museums, although some remain in the hands of the families or private collectors. Paintings are also placed in this category. Although there were official War Artists and Painters their work was seldom repeated, and the paintings themselves also fall in the 'one-of-a-kind' category. In addition, unique things were hand-made or manufactured to honour an event or general.

In this chapter I would like to give the collector a glimpse of the range of rare or one-of-a-kind items which do not normally become available through the usual antique and collectable outlets.

Plate 439
A beautiful silver casket 'Advance Australia'. Engraved: 'Presented to Major General R.S.Baden Powell. By the Residents of Various Municipalities throughout Victoria Australia in commemoration of his gallant defense of Mafeking 1899–1900'.
(*By courtesy of The Scout Association, Baden-Powell House, London*)

Plate 440
A unique silver-gilt casket with a copper cannon and ammunition on top. Around the casket there are fine enamelled pictures. On the top, surrounding the picture of Major-General Baden-Powell, the words '13 Oct 1899 Mafeking Defensor 17 May 1900'. Accompanying the casket there is a certificate which reads: 'To Maj. General R.S.S. Baden Powell. We, the undersigned, on behalf of the Inhabitants of Mafeking, beg to present to you the accompanying Casket in recognition of your gallant services as Officer Commanding during the Siege of the Town by the Boers, Oct 13th 1899 to May 17th 1900'.
(*By courtesy of the The Scout Association, Baden Powell House, London*)

439

440

One-of-a-kind Collectables 219

441

Plate 441
A silver casket with the engraving: 'The Honorary Freedom of the Worshipful Company of Carpenters was presented to the Rt. Hon. Sir Redvers Buller V.C. G.C.B. K.C.M.G. in this casket on March 20, 1901'. Sheffield Silver 1900.

(11 3/16 in. – 30 cm.)

(By courtesy of Major Philip Erskine, Stellenbosch)

442

Plate 442
A silver-gilt casket containing the Freedom of the City of Exeter which was presented to General Buller. The City arms are on the lid, and General Buller's personal arms and his three decorations, V.C., G.C.B., and K.C.M.G., are embossed on the front. The two paintings on enamel are part of a set of four. On the left is Exeter Cathedral and on the right is a street scene. There are two more paintings on the reverse side.
Birmingham Silver 1900.

(11 7/16 in. – 29 cm.)

(By courtesy of Major Philip Erskine, Stellenbosch)

Plate 443
A magnificent enamel and gilt punchbowl and cups next to a sculpted mountain with a mounted Boer on top and armed Boers on the side — known as the 'Bratina' (Brotherhood). The punchbowl is on an elaborately carved wooden stand. The work carries the coats-of-arms of Peter the Great, the Orange Free State and the South African Republic, and the engraving '*Het Russische Volk aan Piet Cronje en zijne Boeren*' (The Russian Nation to Piet Cronje and his Boers).
Sculptor : A. Aubert.

(6 ft. 6 in. – 198 cm.)

(By courtesy of the National Cultural History and Open-Air Museum, Pretoria)

443

444

Plate 444
An enamel and gilt presentation cup presented by the Citizens of the City of Moscow to General Cronje 1900.
(15 in. – 38.1 cm.)
(*By courtesy of the National Cultural History and Open-Air Museum, Pretoria*)

445

Plate 445
A Belgian commemorative from Lier, with the inscription:
'*Aan Kruger en zijn Helden*' (To Kruger and his heroes); '*Hetzij gij overwint Hetzij gij sterft De Vrijheid zal over Zuid-Afrika rijzen Als de zon in de Morgen-wolken*' (Whether you win, or whether you die, the freedom will rise in South Africa like the sun in the morning clouds).
Sculptor: Lodewijk van Boestel, Lier.
(*By courtesy of the National Cultural History and Open-Air Museum, Pretoria*)

Plate 446
A pair of silver spurs marked 'Best Victoria Silver'. The label attached to the spurs reads: 'These spurs were once the property of Gen. Kruger given to Lord Robert's Batman on Kruger's surrender at Pretoria S.A. 1900.

One-of-a-kind Collectables

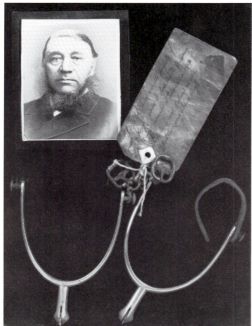
446

447

'The Batman was a Corporal in the 1st Battalion Hampshire Regt.'
(There are inaccuracies in the above, e.g. 'Gen. Kruger' instead of 'Pres. Kruger', while 'Kruger's surrender' should be 'Pretoria's surrender'. This is common in third party reports. Interesting pieces all the same.)
(From the Oosthuizen Collection)

Plate 447
A watercolour of two British artillerymen by Frans D. Oerder (1900).
Frans Oerder was an official War Artist and became one of the best-loved South African artists
$(15\frac{3}{4} \times 12\frac{1}{4}$ in. $- 40 \times 31$ cm.$)$
(By permission of the Africana Museum, Johannesburg)

Plate 448
A painting of a Boer War battle by the famous Boer War artist R. Caton-Woodville.
$(40\frac{1}{2} \times 25$ in. $- 102.9 \times 63.5$ cm.$)$
(From the collection of Mr Kenneth Griffith, London)

448

Plate 449
A fine action sketch of a British soldier on his horse by Major-General Baden-Powell.
$12\frac{1}{2} \times 8\frac{1}{2}$ in. – 31.7 × 21.6 cm.
(*By courtesy of The Scout Association, Baden-Powell House, London*)

Plate 450
'Pretoria Ambulances at Modderrivier Nov. 1899 – Feb 1900' by Frans Oerder, the first official War Artist in South Africa. He travelled with the Boers throughout the war.
(12 × 8 in. – 30.5 × 20.3 cm.)
(*By courtesy of the War Museum of the Boer Republics, Bloemfontein*)

Plate 451
A watercolour sketch of 'Roll Call' in a POW camp in St. Helena by Erich Mayer, the well-known South African artist. A prisoner of war in St. Helena during the Boer War, he made his sketches in St. Helena during his internment and added colour upon his return in South Africa, hence the two dates on the works. Dated 1903.
($5\frac{3}{4} \times 7\frac{11}{16}$ in. – 14.5 × 19.5 cm.)
(*By courtesy of the National Cultural History and Open-Air Museum, Pretoria*)

Plate 452
A watercolour by Erich Mayer of 'Napoleon's House' on St. Helena, with a British soldier and Boer POWs in the foreground.
Dated 1902 and 1903.
($5\frac{1}{8} \times 6\frac{11}{16}$ in. – 13 × 17 cm.)
(*By courtesy of the National Cultural History and Open-Air Museum, Pretoria*)

One-of-a-kind Collectables 223

451

452

453

454

Plate 453
A large oil painting of 'Cronje's Lager at Paardeberg' by G.D. Giles, dated 18th February 1900.
(*By permission of the National Army Museum, London*)

Plate 454
A large oil painting by George Scott of General Buller crossing the Tugela, entitled 'Royal Horse Artillery South Africa 1900'.
(*By permission of the National Army Museum, London*)

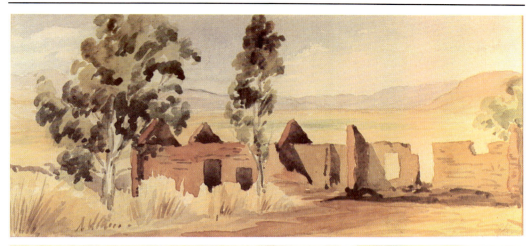

455

456

Plate 455
A watercolour painting by Emily Hobhouse, the British philanthropist, of a farm in Roossenekal in the Transvaal, as left by British troops.
(9 × 4 in. − 22.9 × 10.1 cm.)
(*By courtesy of the War Museum of the Boer Republics, Bloemfontein*)

Plate 456
'Paardeberg', a painting by the German artist Graf.
(*By courtesy of the War Museum of the Boer Republics, Bloemfontein*)

Plate 457

A page from the beautiful diary of Willem A. Baay, a Boer prisoner of war in the Ragama Camp in Ceylon. At the top of the page: 'Ragama Ceylon' and in the centre a 'Good For' note for ten cents issued by The Ceylon Ice & Cold Storage Company for use in their store in the Ragama Camp.
Every page in the diary has different border decorations.
(*By courtesy of the National Cultural History and Open-Air Museum, Pretoria*)

Plate 458

A fine example of an exquisitely decorated commemorative letter from Russia. All Russian cities and towns sent commemorative letters addressed to Boer Generals in specific or to the Boers, or the Boer Nation. Most of them recorded the signatures of the prominent citizens of the town or city and each one was decorated in a different fashion.
(*By courtesy of the National Cultural History and Open-Air Museum, Pretoria*)

One-of-a-kind Collectables

Plate 459
A colourful German stained-glass window in the Kruger House, Pretoria. At the top pictures of Pretoria, Peace and Bloemfontein. In the centre President Kruger and President Steyn flanked by pictures of General Botha and General De Wet above lions.
Below, the coats-of-arms of the South African Republic and the Orange Free State.
(*By courtesy of the National Cultural History and Open-Air Museum, Pretoria*)

Plate 460
A silver flask used by Major-General Baden-Powell in Mafeking during the Siege.
(*By permission of the National Army Museum, London*)

Plate 461
A stone carving of Lord Roberts. Around his image the engraving: 'Field-Marshal Lord Roberts V.C.'.
(*By permission of the National Army Museum, London*)

Plate 462
A large oakwood armchair, made in England. Elaborately carved, with a crest on top with the motto 'Spernit. Pericula. Virtus'. Below

462

464

it, four carved panels of Boer generals: Louis Botha, P.J. Joubert, C. de Wet, and De La Rey.
(height 4 ft. – 122 cm., width 26 in. – 66 cm. seat height 20 in. – 50.8 cm.)
(*By courtesy of the National Cultural History and Open-Air Museum, Pretoria*)

Plate 464
(*See* below) Two Dutch tile tableaux, the first with the coat-of-arms of the Transvaal, the second with the coat-of-arms of the Orange Free State.

Plate 465
(*See* below) A Dutch tile picture of the Boer General J. H. M. Kock.

Plate 466
(*See* below) A large Dutch tile tableaux of the Battle of Colenso.

463

Plate 463
A bronze sculpture entitled 'Sad News' by Anton van Wouw.
(14 in. – 35.5 cm.) (*By courtesy of the War Museum of the Boer Republics, Bloemfontein*)

In the late 1960s a whole collection of historic Boer War Dutch tile tableaux was discovered under the wallpaper of a theatre in Rotterdam in the Netherlands. It was the Transvalia Theatre at the turn of the century. The tiles were made by the 'De Distel' factory in Amsterdam and the painter was Cornelius de Bruin.
The collection is now on permanent display in the War Museum of the Boer Republics in Bloemfontein.

465

466

Index

'Absent-minded Beggar, The' 21, 138, 162, 170, 171, 180, 192, 197
acid-etching 59, 60
addresses 137, 138, 139
advertisements 170–1, 184, 189
Africana Museum, Johannesburg 49, 59, 61, 86, 95, 117, 123, 124, 130, 131, 138, 142, 145, 151, 166, 167, 180, 181, 182, 184, 200, 221
Ahmednagar Fort 88
Aicrette 155
Albemarle, Earl of 181
Alexandra, Queen 16, 177, 209
Allervale Pottery 24
Ally Sloper's Half-holiday 20, 143, 144, 171
Ames, Mr and Mrs E. 189
Ammon of Nuremberg 54
ammunition fragments 199–200
Amsterdam 156, 157, 166, 168, 228
angel 43
Annexation of the South African Republic 171
Antique Collectors' Club 43
armoured train 54, 160, 187
army supply column 54
Ashington 32
ashtray 20, 122, 129, 200, 201
Aubert, A. 219
Australia 163, 182, 193, 217
Austria 24
Avelino A. S. Bello 33

Baay, Willem A. 226

Baden-Powell, Major-General 3, 4, 7, 9, 11, 14, 15, 18, 21, 23, 25, 38, 39, 42, 48, 60, 61, 62, 63, 66, 69, 73, 102, 106, 117, 127, 128, 129, 135, 146, 147, 150, 151, 155, 160, 172, 177, 178, 185, 190, 195, 201, 203, 208, 209, 217, 222, 227
bank notes 102
banks, private 102
banner 187
Barnstaple 38
Bavaria 23
Beaconsfield 77
beaver 3
Bechuanaland Protectorate 66, 69, 102
Beecham's Pills 170
bees 29
Belgium 28, 146, 220
bell 210
Belle Vue Camp 83, 88, 97, 103, 109
Belmont 179
belt 124,
Benbow Collection 90
Benbow, Mr Colin 92
Beresford, Lord Charles 129
Bermingham, Superintendent A. 89, 90, 91, 95
Bermuda 69, 75, 77, 83, 84, 85, 87, 89, 90, 91, 92, 95, 143
Beyers, Commandant 28
Bible 90, 169
Birkbeck, Major 102
biscuit barrel 17, 23
Biscuit Porcelain 48
bisque ware 35, 45, 46

Black Watch 36, 57, 171
blockhouses 139
Bloemfontein 67, 70, 128, 129, 179, 180, 190, 199, 227 (*see also* War Museum of the Boer Republics)
boar 5, 38, 118
'Bobs' 7, 45, 121, 180, 201, 206
Bomm Porzelan Werken 29
bone 85, 92, 94, 95
Bonheur, Theo 154
bookmarks 183, 184
books 189–90
Border Scouts 102, 108
Botenschamp 70
'Botha, General' 11, 94, 124, 130, 146, 159, 207, 227
Botha, Louis 30, 198, 215, 228
bottle 216
bottle cork 210
Bovril 170
Brabant, Brigadier-General 147
braces 98
Brandfort 180
Brannam, R. P., C.H. 38
brass 50, 214, 215
Britannia 2, 128
Britannia Porcelain Works 24
Britain's models 53–4, 58
Britain, William 53
British and Benington's Tea Trading Association Ltd. 127
British West Indies 69, 83
Broad Bottom Camp 138
bronze 49, 50, 192, 196, 197, 198, 228
brooch 94, 95, 114, 116, 199
bulldogs 17
Buller, General Sir Redvers 5, 6, 8, 9, 10, 12, 13, 15, 17, 18, 21, 22, 23, 25, 40, 41, 45, 48, 61, 62, 127, 128, 129, 147, 150, 160, 172, 177, 178, 180, 182, 201, 206, 208, 215, 216, 219, 224
Bull, John 33, 43, 170
bullocks 56
Burt's Island 84, 92, 95, 143
bust 36, 43, 45, 50, 62, 63
buttons 94, 184, 207
Byng, Geo. W. 155

Cadbury, Messrs 131
Cafe Transvalia 63
Canada 4, 9, 160, 182, 189, 192, 193
candlesticks 49, 90
Cape Colony 4, 62, 65, 83, 102, 182
Cape of Good Hope 65, 66, 67, 69, 71, 75, 77, 80, 102, 104

Cape Town 75, 77, 83, 181, 182
card holder 210
Cardigan, Earl of 80
caricatures 162, 163, 165
Carlton Ware 7, 18, 21
Carpenters, Worshipful Company of 219
cartoons 162, 163, 165
caskets 217, 219
cast-iron 201, 202, 203, 214
Caton Woodville, R. 21, 162, 170, 172, 178, 221
Cavalry, Boer 53
cedar, Bermuda 89, 90, 91
celluloid 210
censors' marks 70, 75, 77, 88, 97
ceramics 1, 21, 28, 29, 30, 31, 35, 36, 38
Ceylon 69, 77, 83, 89, 90, 92, 94, 109, 130, 143, 145, 166, 174, 182, 226
Ceylon Ice & Cold Storage Co. Ltd. 109, 226
chain 116
chair 87, 227
Chamberlain, Joseph 20, 36, 147, 151, 159, 165, 168, 171, 175, 177, 180, 208
champagne flute 61
Chapman 6
charm bracelet 117
chocolate box 174
chocolate cards 147
chocolate tins 131, 184
Christian Colour-Sergeant, A. 171
Christmas cards 161
Churchill, Winston 171
cigarette cards 146–7
cigarette case 121, 124
cigarette holder 21
cigarettes 170, 175
City Imperial Volunteers 18, 45, 49, 50, 54, 57, 172, 181, 194, 203, 206, 209
Claase, J. J. 28
Clery, Lieutenant-General Sir C. F. 128, 146, 150, 201
clock 123
Coalport 8
coats-of-arms 11, 12, 30, 32, 33, 60, 65, 88, 89, 90, 92, 95, 113, 115, 118, 121, 123, 124, 130, 132, 160, 182, 183, 184, 185, 187, 200, 203, 204, 219, 227, 228
Cockburn, Lieutenant H. Z. C. 160
coins, 97, 101–2, 103, 104, 110, 113, 114, 115, 116, 118, 122, 124, 165
Colenso 159, 179, 198, 228
Colesberg 179
collage 216
Collins, Arthur 151
Colombo 77, 109
Colonial Trooper 8, 36

Colonies 4, 21, 182
Commandani Camp 83, 85
commemorative letters 137, 138
compass 214
concentration camps 84, 177
Copeland 1, 4, 35, 38
Cornwall, Duke and Duchess of 193
Coventry 177, 178
covers 68–70, 75, 80
'Creaky' 4
Cronje, General 4, 28, 61, 124, 130, 147, 181, 219, 220, 224
Crown Staffordshire 24
cuff-links 114, 115, 117
cups 4, 15, 21, 22, 23, 92, 128, 213, 219, 220
cutlery 113, 118, 120, 124
cut-outs 160, 166, 167

Daily Mail 172, 197
Darrells Island 85, 87
De Aar 80
Deadwood Camps 77, 83, 143
de Bruin, Cornelius 228
De Distel factory 228
Deelfontein 162
De La Rey, General 11, 30, 60, 94, 124, 130, 159, 198, 207, 215, 228
Derby 35
Derbyware 13
de Villebois-Mareuil, Colonel 27, 28, 247
de Villiers Album 92
Devonshire Regiment 54, 77, 131
De Wet, General 11, 28, 30, 31, 42, 94, 128, 130, 139, 159, 187, 198, 200, 207, 215, 227, 228
diary 226
Diyatalawa Camp 77, 92, 109, 143, 145, 172, 174, 182
dogs 4, 17, 38
dolls 210, 211
doll's settee 86
Dominica 69, 83
doorknocker 214
Doulton 2, 3, 36
Douwe Egberts Museum, Utrecht 205
Driefontein 179
Dublin Fusiliers 54, 155
Dudson 25
Dundonald, Lord 39, 117, 147
Durban 77, 80, 83, 92, 115
Dutch items 29, 30, 31, 161, 166, 168, 174, 196, 228 (*see also* Netherlands)
Dutch Red Cross 80

earthenware 3, 17, 28, 31

East Highveld 68, 75
East London 216
East Surrey Regiment 117
Edward VII 16, 66, 67, 68, 128, 177, 192, 195, 203, 209
Eewige Broederband 33
egg cups 23, 92
Elandsfontein 169
Elandslaagte 80, 159, 160, 161, 179
Elkington & Co. Ltd. 48
Ella, Agnes 156
Elliott, London 3
embroidery 183, 184, 187
enamel 215, 219, 220
English Fruit Preserving Company 61, 63
envelopes 69, 75, 77
Erasmus, General 146, 147
Ermelo and Carolina stamps 68, 75
Erskine, Major Philip 14, 17, 22, 25, 63, 85, 219
Essex Regiment 179
etching, acid (on glass) 59, 60
etchings 162, 163, 189
Evans, Archibald 154
Exeter 219

Falcon Factory 35
fan 172
Faulkner C. W. & Co. 160
field notes 102, 106
Field Post Offices 70, 77, 80
flags 2, 3, 5, 6, 7, 8, 9, 13, 16, 24, 29, 60, 61, 97, 129, 153, 163, 177, 179, 180, 183, 187, 204, 207
flask 38, 227
Florentine China 12
Foley China 15
Foley Faience 22
Foley Intarsio 19, 20
Forbes Magazine Museum of Military Miniatures 54, 56, 57
Forestier Walker, Lieutenant-General Sir F. 150
France 27, 29, 47, 63, 143, 144, 146, 151, 153, 167, 173
French, Major-General 3, 7, 8, 11, 15, 21, 23, 40, 121, 127, 128, 129, 134, 147, 150, 160, 172, 177, 184, 195, 201, 208, 209, 214
Fry, J. S. & Sons 131
funeral programme 169

games 88, 95, 110, 124, 165–8
Gatacre, Lieutenant-General Sir William 10, 147, 150
Gemma 32

'Gentleman in Khaki' 21, 45, 49, 61, 118, 121, 122, 124, 131, 133, 162, 172, 177, 178, 197, 203, 210, 214
George, A. 12
Germany 29, 31, 54, 62, 132, 139, 143, 153, 165, 166, 173, 174, 178, 187, 200, 204, 213, 215, 225, 227
Gladstone, W. E. 177, 178
Glasgow Fleming 6
Glasock, Driver 160
glasses 61, 63
glass jar 122
Gloucester Regiment 54
goblet, wine 59
gold 101, 104, 113, 114, 115, 217
Goode, T. and Co. 1
'good fors' 102–3, 108, 109, 226
Goodyear, Sergeant-Major 66
Gordon Highlanders 53
Goss, 32, 35
Government notes 102, 106
Graf 225
Grant, W. H. 177
Green Point Camp 83, 103, 108
greeting cards 158
Grenadier Guards 160
Griffith, Mr Kenneth 4, 12, 18, 19, 20, 27, 32, 38, 43, 45, 47, 50, 62, 80, 87, 92, 97, 124, 128, 129, 133, 135, 142, 147, 151, 160, 165, 166, 172, 184, 199, 201, 203, 204, 211, 213, 221
Griquatown 102
Guardsman 36
guerilla war 70
Gun Hill 122
gunner 160

Hadley's Worcester 36
Hadman, C. 7
Hampshire Regiment 221
handkerchiefs 177, 179, 180, 181, 182
'Handy Man' 3, 9, 16, 36, 45, 46, 50, 118, 129, 133, 147, 172, 210
Hardham, Farrier-Major W. P. 159
harmonica 213
Harris, Henry 56
Hawkin's Island 75
Heilbron 77
Heyde of Dresden 54
Hilyard, Major-General H. J. T. 150
Highlanders 6, 8, 9, 27, 53, 54
Hinks Wells & Co. 213
Hinsons Island 89
HMS *Doris* 54
HMS *Monarch* 54
HMS *Powerful* 16, 54, 116, 206

HMS *Terrible* 4, 54, 159, 199
Hoberman, Gerald 104
Hobhouse, Emily 225
Hohner, M. 213
Holland, *see* Netherlands
Hong Kong 182
horn 87, 92, 213
Hornsby, Major 160
horses 39, 40, 41, 49, 85, 222
hospital ships 190, 204
Hungary, 156
Hunter, Major-General Sir Archibald 150
Hussars 181

identity card 172
illustrations 162
Imperial Forces 36
Imperial Military Railways 162
Imperial Volunteer 2, 6
Imperial Yeomanry 36, 54, 57, 155
India 4, 69, 83, 88, 94, 203
Infantry, Boer 53, 58
    British 56
    South African Mounted 53
internees 183
internment camps 84, 177
inkwell 49, 92
Irish Rifles 57
Italy 153

Jack and the Beanstalk 151
Jacobsdal 181
Jameson, Dr 53
jewellery 94, 95, 101, 113, 114, 115, 116, 117
J.G. &. N., London 13
Johannesburg 77, 129, 162 (*see also* African Museum)
Johannesburg Proclamation 182
Johnson, Peter 54, 56, 57
Joubert, General 11, 25, 28, 29, 124, 147, 158, 168, 174, 180, 204, 228
jug 3, 4, 5, 14, 16, 18, 20, 21, 24, 26, 27, 28, 30, 31, 32, 38

kangaroo 3
Karlsbad 24
Kearsley, Ken 56, 57
Keen, Robinson & Co. Ltd. 129
Kekewich, Colonel 128, 150, 201
Kelly–Kenny, General 117, 127, 147, 150, 201, 208
Kimberley 48, 69, 103, 128, 142, 161, 179, 180, 183, 199
Kings Lynn 195
Kinnears Handicap Cigarettes 170
Kipling Poem War Fund 197

Kipling, Rudyard 21, 170, 171, 172, 180
Kitchener, Lord 8, 9, 10, 11, 13, 14, 15, 18, 19, 20, 21, 23, 25, 31, 36, 40, 42, 45, 50, 61, 63, 80, 92, 121, 127, 128, 129, 132, 134, 147, 150, 155, 159, 160, 172, 177, 178, 201, 208, 209, 213, 215
knife-rest 199
Knight, Aldershot 5
knives 94, 113, 199, 200
Kock, General Jan 147, 228
Koffyfontein 103, 111
Komati River 160
Kornspruit 160
Krijgsgevangene 70, 88
Kroonstad 180
Kruger House 153, 227
Kruger, Mrs 144
Kruger, President 8, 14, 17, 19, 22, 23, 24, 25, 26, 27, 28, 30, 31, 33, 36, 38, 50, 59, 60, 62, 63, 85, 91, 97, 101, 104, 110, 115, 124, 132, 144, 146, 147, 151, 156, 159, 163, 165, 168, 170, 171, 173, 175, 177, 178, 179, 180, 184, 187, 196, 197, 198, 200, 203, 204, 205, 207, 208, 210, 213, 215, 220, 221, 227
Kruitzinger, Commandant 147
Küpfer, Wilhelm 174

Ladysmith 9, 13, 15, 69, 77, 80, 83, 116, 128, 129, 143, 145, 147, 161, 169, 178, 179, 180, 183, 184, 199, 203
Lambeth 2, 3, 36
Lambton, Captain H. 3
lamps 47
Lancashire Fusilier 56
Lancers 9, 160, 182
Langs-Nek 161
lapel pins 207, 208, 209
Lawton, W. C. 43, 45
lead 135
leopard 88
le Roux, W. 183
Lessard, Lieutenant-Colonel F. L. 189
letter-opener 122, 210
letters 137, 138, 171
Lier 220
Life Guards 160
Light Infantry 160
Lindley 199
linen 182
lion 3, 5, 13, 87, 88, 124, 129, 151, 163, 208, 227
lithographs 162
Lockhart, David and Sons 9
Lodge, Gunner 160
London Regiment 160
Long, M. H. 163

Longton 11, 32
loving cup 1, 2, 3, 24
Lucas, Henri 158
lustre ware 11, 12, 19, 22, 23

Maastricht 31
Macdonald, General Hector 8, 9, 23, 39, 41, 127, 147, 150, 172, 177, 201
Machadodorp 77
Macintyre, James & Co. Ltd. 21
Mafeking 3, 4, 9, 15, 42, 48, 60, 61, 66, 69, 73, 102, 103, 105, 106, 128, 129, 135, 147, 153, 154, 161, 178, 179, 180, 183, 190, 199, 203, 217, 227
magazines 143, 144–5, 163, 171, 189
Magersfontein 159, 161, 171, 178
magic lantern slides 211
Mahon, Colonel 3
Majuba 20
maps 135, 142, 163, 180
marble 35, 50
March, Sidney 48
March, Vernon 49
marine 4, 48, 50 (*see also* Royal Marine)
Maritz 139
Marks, Sammy 104
Martin-Leake, Surgeon-Captain A. 159
match covers 201
match holder 13, 21, 22, 199
Mayer, Erich 138, 222
medallions 190, 192, 193, 194, 195, 196, 198, 199, 215
medals 190, 192, 196, 197
meerschaum 203
Methuen, Lord 128, 147, 150, 201, 208, 209
militaria 199
Mills, Mr Lawrence 87
Milner, Sir A. 147
Mink, Max & Co. 115
Modder River 168, 222
model soldiers 53–8
money box 38, 50, 199
monkey 171
Morgans Island 86
Moscow 220
moustache cup 23
Mozambique 24, 84
mug, 12, 13, 16, 24, 132
Mullins, Captain C. E. 160
music 153–8, 180
music box 215

Naaunport 159
Natal 4, 31, 48, 54, 66, 70, 71, 80, 83, 102, 124, 129, 161

National Army Museum, London 7, 13, 46, 48, 85, 89, 94, 95, 105, 117, 131, 139, 140, 144, 145, 155, 160, 162, 163, 168, 181, 182, 184, 185, 190, 192, 193, 194, 195, 199, 205, 206, 209, 210, 225, 227
National Cultural History and Open Air Museum, Pretoria 11, 12, 22, 23, 25, 29, 30, 31, 38, 60, 62, 75, 88, 90, 94, 95, 97, 98, 99, 108, 109, 111, 124, 130, 145, 156, 157, 158, 161, 169, 173, 174, 183, 187, 198, 199, 204, 205, 207, 210, 219, 220, 222, 226, 227, 228
Naudee's Kop 122
naval gun 54, 56
naval landing party 53, 54, 56
needle box 86
Netherlands 31, 143, 153, 156, 157, 158, 228 (*see also* Dutch items)
Newark 195
New South Wales 4, 9, 160, 182
newspapers 143, 144–5, 153, 163, 171, 197
New Testament 169
New Zealand 4
Nile (Hospital Ship) 204
Northumberland Fusiliers 203
nurse 46, 124
nutcracker 213

oakwood 227
Oerder, Frans 221, 222
official documents 171
Ogden 146
Oliver, General 147
Oom, Paul 26, 38, 124, 163
Orange Free State Republic 8, 12, 24, 28, 30, 31, 60, 67, 71, 75, 77, 89, 97, 102, 104, 107, 115, 118, 135, 180, 183, 184, 187, 200, 204, 219, 227, 228
Orange River Colony 8, 12, 67, 71, 84
orange tree 67
Ossulston-Rich, Riche 184
ostrich 3
oxen 85, 101

Paardeberg 20, 88, 179, 224, 225
Paardekop 162
paintings 89, 217, 221, 224, 225
paperclip 215
paper knife 89, 92
paperweights 62, 90
Parian ware 35, 43, 45
Paris 59
Parker, Sergeant 160
passes 162
patchwork 183
peace 16, 43, 128, 153, 169, 181, 227

Peace, Lady 11, 12, 24
peace music album 154
pendants 114, 115, 117, 192
pens 213
perfume bottle 25
permits 162
Peter the Great 219
pewter 18, 25, 127, 132, 135
Phillips 54, 58
photographs 139, 140, 189, 211, 214
picture frames 89, 90, 121, 133, 135
Pietermaritzburg 124, 161
Pietersburg 68, 75, 102, 106
Pietershill 179
Pijper, T. 157
Pilgrims Rest 102
pin cushion 210
Pioneer Tobacco 170
pipe bowl 205, 206
pipe rack 204
pipes 203, 204, 205, 207
pipe tray 21, 22
place-card holder 124
plaques 10, 12, 197
plates 1, 5, 6, 7, 8, 9, 11, 27, 28, 29, 31, 60, 95, 127, 128
playing cards 166
Plumer, Colonel 147, 150, 201
Pöcher, Guido 156
pocket knife 199, 200
Pole Carew, Major-General 127
porcelain 1, 4, 11, 14, 15, 16, 17, 24, 25, 29, 35, 36, 38, 204, 205
Port Elizabeth 77
Portland, Duke of 32
Portugal 28, 29, 33, 84, 153
postal orders 102
postcards 77, 158, 159, 160, 161
posters 137, 138, 147, 150, 151, 153, 211
postmarks 70
pottery 1, 13, 26
powder horn 30
prayers 169
pressed-glass 59, 60
Pretoria 2, 3, 48, 60, 68, 70, 75, 77, 80, 83, 89, 106, 124, 129, 132, 142, 143, 144, 145, 151, 153, 161, 167, 169, 172, 179, 180, 182, 190, 193, 203, 220, 222, 227 (*see also* National Cultural History and Open Air Museum)
Pretorius, Commandant H. 147
Prince of Wales 147
prisoner-of-war camps 69–70, 75, 77, 83–99, 102–3, 108–9, 138, 143, 144, 145, 153, 157, 163, 166, 172, 174, 177, 182, 199, 203, 222, 226

programmes 169, 173, 174
Punch 165
punchbowl 219

Queensland 4, 182

Ragama 83, 109, 166, 226
rail tickets 162
Read, Ezra 154
Red Cross 70, 80, 172
Regout, Petrus & Co. 31
Rensburg 179
Rhodes, Cecil 27, 49, 129, 163
Roberts, Lieutenant F. 147, 159
Roberts, Lord 3, 4, 5, 6, 7, 8, 9, 11, 13, 15, 16, 18, 19, 20, 21, 23, 25, 40, 41, 42, 43, 45, 46, 48, 50, 60, 61, 68, 89, 117, 121, 122, 124, 127, 128, 129, 130, 132, 134, 146, 147, 150, 151 155, 160, 163, 171, 172, 177, 178, 179, 180, 181, 182, 190, 192, 193, 195, 201, 203, 206, 208, 209, 213, 214, 215, 220, 227
Robertson, Sergeant-Major William 159
Roehlin, L. 132
rolling-pin 61
Roossenekal 225
rosette 184
Ross, E. J. 190
Rotterdam 63, 228
Rousseau 47
Rowntree, Messrs 131
Royal Engineers' Observation Section 57
Royal Horse Artillery 224
Royal Horse Guards 160
Royal Marine 2, 3, 9, 16, 45, 160
Royal Navy 9, 16, 160
Royal Sussex Regiment 171
Royal Vale China 11
Royal Worcester 36
Rundle, Lieutenant-General Sir Leslie 128, 201
Russell & Sons 7
Russia 137, 153, 219, 220
Rustenburg 31, 68

salt cellar 135
Sanna's Post 163
Sarreguemines 26, 28
sash 184, 185
sauce boat 28
saucer 15, 22, 23
Schaul, Corporal J. 159
Schiel, General 147
Schoeman, General H. 147
Schoonhoven 29
Schumann, J. H. L. 157
Schweizer Reinecke 68

scissors 200
Scott, Captain P. M. 3
Scott, Fabian 154
Scott, George 224
Scout Association 38, 106, 153, 185, 190, 217, 222
sculpture 228
seals 75, 77
sermons 169
serviette ring 86, 95, 122
Sheldon, C. M. 163
shirt stud 215
shoulder band 184, 185
signatures 171, 183
silk 183, 184
silver 88, 101, 102, 103, 104, 110, 113, 115, 116, 117, 118, 120, 121, 122, 124, 190, 198, 217, 219, 220, 227
Simonstown 83, 97, 109
Singer's 184
Sirdar, The 10
sketches 222
Skirmisher Bright Flake 129
'Small Book' 171
Smuts, General 139
Smythe, Rita & Ian 6, 14, 28, 43, 48, 62, 131, 172
snake 86, 90
Snyman, General 147
soap powder tin 129
Societe Ceramique Maastricht 31
soldiers 4, 7, 9, 12, 13, 14, 15, 16, 17, 18, 21, 36, 46, 47, 49, 118, 129, 133, 135, 139, 165, 178, 201, 222
 model 53–8
songs 157, 172, 173
Sotheby's 49, 61, 63, 73, 89, 105, 123, 132, 204
soup tickets 103
South African Mounted Infantry 53
South African Republic 8, 11, 26, 67, 68, 72, 75, 77, 80, 85, 89, 90, 92, 97, 102, 103, 104, 106, 113, 114, 115, 116, 118, 122, 124, 130, 132, 180, 182, 185, 203, 204, 219, 227
spelter 47, 50
Spink & Son 197
Spion Kop 122, 179
Spode 4, 38
Spoel, Arnold 157
spurs 220
Sri Lanka, *see* Ceylon
Staffordshire 35, 39, 40, 41, 42, 43
stained-glass window 227
stamps 65–8, 71, 72, 73, 75, 77, 80
Standard Bank 102
stationery, Red Cross 80

St. Buryan, Cornwall 13
Stellaland 66
Stevengraphs 177, 178, 179
Stevens, T, 177, 178
Steyn, M. T., President 30, 33, 60, 63, 146, 147, 168, 183, 198, 215, 227
St. Helena 69, 77, 83, 86, 87, 91, 95, 138, 140, 143, 157, 199, 222
St. John's, Order of 195
Stoke-on-Trent 7, 13, 16, 18, 20, 35
stone carvings 90, 92, 207, 227
stoneware 25
sugar bowl 24
Sullivan, Arthur 180
Swaziland 67
Symons, General Sir, W. P. 150

tables 202, 203
Taddy's 146, 147
Talana 122
tampers 203
Tangier 54, 56, 57
tape-measures 134, 210
tapestry 185, 187
Tasmania 4
Taylor, T. H. 13
Taylor, Tunnicliffe & Co. Ltd., Hanly 14
tea caddy 127, 130
tea canister 127, 130
tea cards 147
teapots 18, 19, 20, 21
teapot stands 10, 11
tea-sets 15, 22
Terre de Fer 27
Te Velde notes 102, 106
textiles 97–9, 177–87
tickets 162
ties 98, 99
tiles 10, 228
tin, 124, 127, 128, 129, 130, 131, 134
Tin Town Camp 77, 83
Tipping, Mr Brian 203
tobacco 170
tobacco jar 17, 18, 23, 31, 38, 86
tobacco tin 131
'Tommy Atkins' 118, 144
tortoise 92
tot measure 210
toys 88
Trade Brothers 16
Transvaal 12, 24, 27, 31, 32, 50, 60, 66, 67, 68, 72, 75, 77, 80, 83, 84, 88, 95, 97, 102, 115, 121, 124, 135, 183, 184, 187, 200, 225, 228
Transvalia Theatre 228
tray 21, 30, 121, 129

trench art 199
trick boxes 86, 90
trivets 214
Tugela 122, 224
tumblers 15, 16, 30, 60, 61, 63

Uitlanders 129
umbrella stands 201
Union Jack 179, 180, 182
'Unity is strength' 2 11, 12, 16, 29, 85, 90, 132, 174, 179, 197, 200, 203, 204
Upington 102, 108
Urry, Mr R. 102
USA 50, 77, 84, 153, 190
US Consulate 77
Utrecht 205

Vaal River 139, 162, 180
van Boestel, Lodewijk 220
van den Eijnde 156
Van Deventer 139
Van Schoch & Co. 31
van Wouw, Anton 228
vases 14, 21, 25
Veldpond 104, 114
Veldpost 70
vesta 121, 134, 214
Victoria 4, 217
Victoria Cross 6, 146, 147, 159
Victoria, Queen 1, 2, 3, 4, 12, 22, 62, 66, 90, 128, 131, 144, 146, 151, 165, 177, 180, 184, 203, 208, 209
viewer 211
viewing cards 211
Villeroy & Bosch 28
Villiers 11
Vlakfontein 159
Vryburg 66
Volunteers 21
vulcanite 214

walking sticks 87
wall plaques 10, 12
War Artists 217, 221, 222
War Museum of the Boer Republics, Bloemfontein 28, 33, 63, 75, 77, 85, 92, 99, 107, 113, 114, 118, 120, 122, 124, 138, 139, 153, 168, 174, 175, 178, 179, 183, 184, 187, 207, 215, 216, 222, 225, 228
Warren, Lieutenant-General Sir Chas 150, 201
watch 116, 124
watch chain 94
watercolour 221, 222, 225
Wauchope, Major-General 128, 177, 178
Waugh, F. J. 163
Webbe, Lloyd 87

Wedgwood 19
Werner, Max 155
Westminster Gazette 50
Wheeler, G. D. 155
White, Lieutenant-General Sir George 9, 11, 13, 15, 18, 19, 21, 22, 23, 45, 80, 118, 128, 129, 147, 150, 160, 172, 180, 201, 203, 208, 209
Wilhelmina, Queen 204
Willette, A. 187
William Bros. 9
Williamsons 16
Willow Art China 32
Wills, W. D. & H. O. 146
Wiltshar & Robinson Ltd. 7, 13, 18, 21

With the Flag to Pretoria 170
Wolmaranstad 68
Women's Work Exchange, Bermuda 84
wood carvings 85, 86, 87, 88, 89, 90, 91, 92
Worcester 1, 36

York and Lancaster Regiment 53
York, Duke and Duchess of 193

Zackon, J. D. and C. C. 118, 121
ZAR, *see* South African Republic
Zonatura Tea 130
Zulus 27
Zweers, Bernard 158